ENDORSEMENTS

This authoritative devotional by Brenda Kunneman is destined to equip believers for victory in these especially trying times. There is no better way to face your greatest fears and disappointments than what you'll find in *The Daily Decree*. Get ready for divine favor to invade your life!

—Paul Jr. and Brenda Crouch

Only a prophet who hears clearly from God could have assembled these right-on-target declarations. Starting the day with one declaration from this book will change your day, your life, your family, and your destiny!

—Sid Roth
Host, *It's Supernatural!*

The words that come out of our mouths can shift the atmosphere, unleash our destiny, and change the world! In *The Daily Decree,* Brenda Kunneman equips us to prophetically crush the pathetic with the power of anointed expressions of faith.

—Reverend Samuel Rodriguez
New Season Christian Worship Center
National Hispanic Christian Leadership Conference
Sacramento, CA

The Daily Decree is an amazing book that will encourage and equip you with faith-filled declarations to pray and speak over your life daily. It will empower you to live every day with hope and joy even through the challenges of life. I highly recommend Brenda Kunneman's book to you.

—Lisa Osteen Comes
Author, *You Are Made For More!*

Brenda Kunneman has written an important book that gives a biblically based set of daily declarations. Pastor Kunneman has lived an exemplary life using the principles written in *The Daily Decree*. This work is a must read in this season of spiritual shaking. These declarations are an excellent starting point to increase the spiritual authority and effectiveness of our personal prayer lives. In my circles I will use this book to train both new and mature believers.

—Bishop Harry Jackson, Jr.
Hope Christian Church, Beltsville, Maryland
High Impact Leadership Coalition

We believe that *The Daily Decree* by Brenda Kunneman will greatly enhance your spiritual walk with God. We have said for years, "Nothing happens in the Kingdom without declaration." This book equips you with promises from God's Word to declare as you pray every day. The Bible teaches us that angels give heed to the voice of His word. In other words, the heavenly realm waits with anticipation for you to discover your voice. *The Daily Decree* puts His word right into your hands. Brenda Kunneman masterfully equips you with the written Word of God coupled with prophetic directives that will lead you into a victorious daily walk.

—David & Nicole Binion
Lead Pastors and Recording Artists
Dwell Church, Dallas TX

Pastor Brenda Kunneman's lifestyle of prayer, consecration, and devotion makes her an exceptional example of someone who lives daily in the presence of God. She has discovered that any endeavor is likely to succeed when you simply follow the rules that govern that pursuit. The Bible gives us proven guidelines that govern the subject of prayer—one of the most powerful weapons in our spiritual arsenal. Those who have the most consistent and effective prayer lives are the ones who take advantage of those foundational truths in the word of God. For instance, Isaiah 55:11 promises us that God's word will not return to Him void or empty but *will* accomplish its purpose!

Today, much of what the Body of Christ calls prayer is nothing more than a litany of complaints and a compilation of faithless requests with an "amen" tacked on. In her book *The Daily Decree,* Brenda Kunneman shares scriptural principles for you to declare what God has already said about you and your situation. Instead of lamenting how things are, you should be proclaiming how they will be! This incredible book is a great resource to exponentially increase your effectiveness in prayer.

—Dr. Rod Parsley
Pastor and Founder, World Harvest Church
Columbus, Ohio

As human beings made in the image and likeness of God, we are "meaning makers." We observe life as it unfolds, and internally we interpret what we observe and bring those interpretations to speech. We live in language. We perform linguistic acts on a daily basis, often moment by moment. We talk our way into and out of situations, relationships, and obligations. Language shapes our cultural reality, and our cultural realities shape our language. Whether we are fully paying attention to our linguistic actions or not, we are at times making assertions and at other times making declarations. Whether or not it is an assertion or a declaration is dependent upon our assessment of what we are dealing with.

We are "assessors" and "declarers" by nature, by human nature. We have needs because we are creatures that are dependent on both God and others. God made us intentionally with needs. How we get those needs met is really important. We deeply desire that when promises are made to us, they are kept. We also know that when we make promises to others we need to keep them, or there are consequences in those relationships. The Good News is that God, our Father, has made many, many precious and magnificent promises so that by them we might become partakers of the divine nature. Peter tells us that in his second epistle.

In the midst of having our needs, we make assessments as well as declarations. If we make promises that we know we need to keep, how much more is the God of Truth, who makes promises, loyally loving to keep those promises? Wouldn't wisdom be to fill our hearts with those promises so that when we assess what we are facing, aware of the needs we have that are intended to be met, the declarations we make be rooted in God's "precious and magnificent" promises? God is often saying, "Open your mouth wide that I might fill it!" What does He want our mouth to be filled with? The language of promise! Our speech acts can be overflowing with declarations of what the God of Truth has promised us.

Pastor Brenda Kunneman has done it again by providing us a great little tool—a host of promises from Scripture that we can learn how to bring to speech as "decrees" (which are declarations based on assessments we make in light of God's perspective on life situations). Learning how to shape our speech in relation to the promises of God is quite healthful and beneficial. It is something you want to do daily. Pastor Brenda's brand-new *The Daily Decree* is a tool, an aid, and a guide to help shape your speech-acts, rooted in your assessments that form declarations that are grounded in God's sure promises. There is a daily decree for each and every day. Today might be the best day to start using this wonderful aid to help you navigate your journey by the words of your mouth and the meditations of your heart.

—Bishop Mark J. Chironna
Church On The Living Edge
Mark Chironna Ministries
Longwood, Florida

THE
DAILY
DECREE

DESTINY IMAGE BOOKS
BY BRENDA KUNNEMAN

The Daily Prophecy

The Roadmap to Divine Direction

Decoding Hell's Propaganda

THE

DAILY DECREE

BRINGING YOUR DAY INTO ALIGNMENT WITH
GOD'S PROPHETIC DESTINY

BRENDA KUNNEMAN

DESTINY IMAGE® PUBLISHERS, INC.

P.O. Box 310, Shippensburg, PA 17257-0310

"Promoting Inspired Lives."

This book and all other Destiny Image and Destiny Image Fiction books are available at Christian bookstores and distributors worldwide.

Cover design by Eileen Rockwell

For more information on foreign distributors, call 717-532-3040.

Reach us on the Internet: www.destinyimage.com.

ISBN 13 TP: 978-0-7684-4789-7

ISBN 13 eBook: 978-0-7684-4790-3

ISBN 13 HC: 978-0-7684-4871-9

ISBN 13 LP: 978-0-7684-4791-0

For Worldwide Distribution, Printed in the U.S.A.

TP   10 11 12 13 / 23 22 21 20

HC   1 2 3 4 5 6 7 8 / 23 22 21 20 19

DEDICATION

*I am dedicating this book to my loving
and supportive husband, Hank Kunneman,
who has not only always pushed me to be
all that God has called me to be but has
always encouraged me to spend the time
writing prophetic decrees that will be a
resource of hope for God's people.*

CONTENTS

Preface—19

Your Energy Is Renewed!—23

Virtue and God's Presence upon You!—25

Divinely Set Up—27

Deliverance from the Arrows—29

The Broken Heart Healed—31

Questions Answered—33

Rise Up as an Overcomer!—35

Dedication Renewed; Condemnation Broken—37

Declaring Same-day Miracles!—39

A Double Portion Anointing!—41

A Word in Your Mouth—43

Mighty Warrior Arise!—45

Your Eyes Are Open—47

Declaring Wholeness—49

Your Season of Expansion and Advancement!—51

God Is Granting You Boldness—53

Fire and Passion Ignited—55

Purpose and Destiny Revived—57

Free from Discouragement—59

Fresh Insight and Discernment—61

Blessings upon Your House—63

Marked for Favor!—65

Declare a New Season—67

Decree over Your Occupation and Business—69

Binding Up Weariness—71

Undoing Heavy Burdens!—73

Invading Fear Must Go!—75

Binding Up Troubling Spirits—77

Hope Restored!—79

Prophetic Insight—81

Joy in Knowing Him!—83

Anointed and Appointed!—85

Restoration and Payback!—87

Mental Oppression Is Bound—89

Divine Reversal!—91

Challenging Places Eased—93

Fresh Inspiration and Vision—95

Unexpected Blessings and Surprises!—97

No Weapon of Lies Can Prosper!—99

Strength to Forgive—101

A Keen Ear to Hear—103

Joy and Laughter—105

A Deep Cleansing—107

Immeasurable Peace—109

Another Level of Growth—111

Mountains Removed!—113

Financial Provision Comes Now!—115

Angels Descending and Surrounding—117

Your Fruitful Season Begins Now—119

Overwhelming Love of the Father—121

Relationships Healed and Restored—123

Visions and Dreams from God—125

Restful Sleep—127

Open Doors and Divine Appointments—129

Encounters with His Glory—131

Satisfied with Long, Abundant Life—133

New Realms of Prayer—135

Set Apart as a Holy Vessel—137

Divine Health Rests Upon You—139

A Fresh Confidence—141

Manifesting Signs and Wonders!—143

Divine Endurance—145

A Song in Your Heart—147

Safe Travel and Transit—149

A Sword in Your Mouth!—151

Trusted Friendships—153

Strong and Resilient—155

No Fear of Man—157

Instruction and Intelligence—159

Unity with the Body of Christ—161

Declaration for Israel—163

Prodigals Returning—165

Free from the Curse—167

A Well-Deserved Break!—169

His Perfect Will—171

Never Forsaken—173

New Identity—175

Born to Stand Out—177

Time for a Praise Break!—179

Life More Abundant—181

No More Shame—183

His Body and Blood—185

The Living Word of God—187

Anticipating His Coming—189

Assured Faith—191

A Sharp Memory—193

A Complete Work—195

Authority and Dominion—197

Thoughts of Purity and Virtue—199

Declaration for Friends and Family—201

It Will Come To Pass!—203

A Ready Answer—205

Extraordinary and Unique Miracles—207

Soft and Gentle Words—209

No More Disappointment—211

An Enduring Patience—213

The Enemy Must Flee!—215

Heavenly Rains—217

Right on Time!—219

Promote His Goodness—221

About Brenda Kunneman—223

PREFACE

SOMETIMES we minimize the power of prayer when we tell people that prayer is just a conversation with God and we don't put any parameters on what that means. Sure, prayer is a conversation with a real and caring God, and offering this as a starting place for a new believer on how to pray is a good thing. However, Jesus taught certain rules and parameters for prayer. In Luke 11:1 a disciple asked Jesus to *teach them how* to pray. They obviously understood that prayer was a conversation with God, but they recognized that there are certain rules that govern effective prayer. They understood that one cannot enter their prayer closet and just speak however they feel or say whatever comes to mind and expect to get definitive answers.

When it comes to prayer there are certain things God listens to and others things that He doesn't. Proverbs 28:9 says, "God detests the prayers of a person who ignores the law" (NLT). In other words, God doesn't hear the prayers of a person who ignores His Word or promises during prayer.

Hebrews 11:6 also reminds us that God isn't pleased when a person approaches Him without confident faith. The point is, if we are going to be effective in prayer we need to be saying the kinds of things that God listens to. God doesn't want us coming to Him with a barrage of complaints, negative statements, or expressions of fear. Part of what makes an effective prayer life is repeating His promises back to Him with assurance. God already knows the negatives and fears we may be facing and it does no good for us to spend time telling God what He already knows about our situation. He wants us to step beyond those challenges when we come to Him in prayer because that is what releases His hand to move on our behalf. What will cause God to respond is when we express our confidence in what He has already promised.

Right words are not only important in prayer, they are important to life in general. Proverbs 18:21 says the very power of life and death itself is found in what we say. So if both prayer and our life overall are dependent on using our words effectively, then we should make a habit of speaking and declaring the right things.

The Daily Decree is a collection of biblically based declarations that you can speak over your life. In effect, they are a form of praying and simply speaking right words all in one. Another powerful element regarding prayer is found in the power of agreement. Jesus said when two or more agree while touching anything in prayer it will be done (see Matt. 18:19). You will find this collection of declarations written in such a way that I and others are standing in agreement with you expecting what is being declared to happen. Together, *we* are decreeing what *we* expect to take place! In this way you aren't just speaking it alone, but know that someone is agreeing with what you are saying.

I am convinced that when we speak faith-filled words aloud into the atmosphere that those words go into effect. In fact, declared words when they are based on Bible promises also cause angels to go into action (see Ps. 103:20).

My prayer is that *The Daily Decree* will be an ongoing resource in your life to help you keep putting forth the right words that will not only dispel the works of darkness but help set your course and form your future. There is power in your mouth and things always shift for the better when *we decree!*

YOUR ENERGY
IS RENEWED!

DECLARATION

TODAY, in the spirit of divine agreement, we decree that your youth is being renewed like the eagle. You shall run and not grow weary and you will walk and not faint. Together, we speak over you energy, vitality, life, and longevity. We break off your life the effects of lethargy, exhaustion, and fatigue. We say that all your emotional and bodily functions, systems, hormones, cells, and organs operate properly as they were created by God and shall not cause you to be tired or worn out. We bind up all stress-causing circumstances that would make you weary and we say that they are replaced by seasons of joy unspeakable and full of glory. Right now we declare that the life of God flows through your entire being in a fresh new way and revitalized energy rests upon you now! Amen!

SCRIPTURE

But they that wait upon the Lord shall renew their strength; they shall mount up with wings as eagles; they shall run, and not be weary; and they shall walk, and not faint (Isaiah 40:31).

WORD OF ENCOURAGEMENT

Sometimes when we go through seasons where we feel a lack of energy, we can often feel like giving up in our faith in the areas where we are trusting God for answers to prayer. Of course, a lack of energy can arise from multiple sources ranging from medical issues, financial stress, family challenges, and more. However, God promises to renew our youth and vitality in every situation. A renewal of our physical and emotional energy is something we should actively and regularly trust God to provide in our lives. I want to encourage you today to call upon the Lord and ask Him to renew your energy and vitality as you walk through the busyness and even difficulties of life. It's God's promise to give you strength and energy, so I decree you receive renewed energy and strength today! Don't give up; it's going to work out for your good!

VIRTUE AND GOD'S PRESENCE UPON YOU!

DECLARATION

TODAY we decree together that you experience encounters with God's tangible presence. We say that your mind, heart, and physical being feels and senses the power of the Almighty. May your bones be filled with supernatural life. We call upon the Lord to touch you in an unusual way and that a fresh anointing comes upon you. May the hand of God be upon you everywhere you go. We say that every place you walk this day the glory of the Lord shall go before you, stand beside you, and also be your protection from behind. Even as the anointing of the Lord was with Jesus, so shall that same anointing be upon you. We prophesy that heavenly gifts shall rest upon you and that you are enabled to manifest the Kingdom of heaven in all your circles of influence. We declare right now that you shall surely say, "The presence of the Lord follows me, is here with me and upon me!" Amen!

SCRIPTURE

How God anointed Jesus of Nazareth with the Holy Ghost and with power: who went about doing good, and healing all that were oppressed of the devil; for God was with him (Acts 10:38).

WORD OF ENCOURAGEMENT

Probably one of the greatest desires of every believer is to sense the presence of God upon their lives. While that doesn't necessarily always mean we feel God upon us physically, we can certainly go about our daily lives with the strong awareness that He is there. When we press in with an expectation to experience His presence, we should expect it to manifest. Whether it comes upon our mind, emotions, in our spirit, or even upon our five physical senses, learn to anticipate the manifest presence of God to rest upon you and to be working on your current situation with the manifestation of a miracle!

DIVINELY
SET UP

DECLARATION

Today we decree you come into the place of a divine setup. We decree right now that you begin to see the Lord arranging, rearranging, shifting, and changing circumstances for your good. We say right now that your eyes are opened to see that God is at work in the most difficult situations. We call for a divine revelation to come upon you, enabling you to see the myriad of angels moving on your behalf at this very moment. We declare that you are able to see God setting things in order. We break the power of setback and decline. We command every spirit of hindrance and resistance to be bound in Jesus' Name. We call upon the Lord to make the way so you can go forward in victory and that all things shall work out and turn out well. Right now, we prophesy you are being divinely set up to prosper and succeed! Amen!

SCRIPTURE

And we know that all things work together for good to them that love God, to them who are the called according to his purpose (Romans 8:28).

WORD OF ENCOURAGEMENT

Every person can face times in life when it seems they are experiencing setback. It can feel as though progress made is canceled out by progress lost, and that you wake up in the morning to feel your life or circumstances are no better than the day before. This is one of the most common lies of the enemy. He doesn't want you to see that regardless of how things appear, God is *always* working behind the scenes and setting up unseen situations for your benefit. The Lord is the master planner, and we can always trust that He is working on every problem, every struggle and challenge even when we don't see it. Know today that what may feel like nothing more than another setback, the Spirit of God is also working to divinely set you up for break-through and blessing!

DELIVERANCE FROM THE ARROWS

DECLARATION

TODAY we decree that you are covered by God's mighty angelic forces and delivered from every arrow of the enemy. We prophesy no weapon formed against you shall prosper. We say every diabolical scheme, plot, or plan of the enemy is stopped and interrupted by warring angels and God's power, and every attack must fall to the ground. We say you are delivered from the terror by night and from the arrow that flies by the day. Every pestilence that walks in darkness around you is stopped. We declare no witchcraft curse, no demonic spell, no work of divination, no incantation or hex will have any effect on you and is rendered entirely powerless in the authority of Jesus' Name! And right now, we say every attack is replaced with peace and calm. We say blessing overtakes you and brings all chaos into divine order. We prophesy that you dwell in safety, for the Lord is your refuge. Angels are bearing you up in their hands this day and long life and salvation are upon you! Amen!

SCRIPTURE

Do not be afraid of the terrors of the night, nor the arrow that flies in the day (Psalm 91:5 NLT).

WORD OF ENCOURAGEMENT

One of the greatest things we can be thankful for is God's promise of deliverance and protection. No matter what plot the devil might try, God has a counter-plan available to interrupt the works of darkness. The Bible reminds us to resist the devil and he will flee (see James 4:7). Scripture also says that through our faith and assurance we can quench every fiery arrow of the wicked one (see Eph. 6:16). Make a point to resist the devil through your declaration of faith that the enemy is powerless to inflict evil and tragedy upon your life. Rest in that today and know that you are delivered from the arrows of darkness!

THE BROKEN
HEART HEALED

DECLARATION

TODAY we decree that your heart and soul is mended from all brokenness, turmoil, and pain. We call for an anointing to heal the brokenhearted and mend all your wounds. We ask Jesus, the Great Physician, to restore you from the pain arising from loss, betrayal, mistreatment, abuse, and loneliness. We say that all tormenting memories are erased from your mind. We command the spirit of fear that would come to make you apprehensive about your future is bound in the Name of Jesus! We declare the negative events of the past have no more power to harass, haunt, or take up residence in your thoughts. We speak inner peace and emotional wholeness over you and that assurance, confidence, and faith arise within you to replace all past brokenness. We speak a mighty and divine healing upon you now!

SCRIPTURE

The Spirit of the Lord is upon me, because he hath anointed me to preach the gospel to the poor; he hath sent me to heal the brokenhearted, to preach deliverance to the captives, and recovering of sight to the blind, to set at liberty them that are bruised (Luke 4:18).

WORD OF ENCOURAGEMENT

One of Jesus' key purposes on earth was to heal. He not only healed the physically infirm, but His pronouncement about His own call and ministry was to heal those suffering from a broken heart. Having one's heart broken as a result of disappointment, betrayal, or loss affects every aspect of a person's life. The Lord doesn't want you living internally broken today. Jesus came to supply abundant life (see John 10:10), which means being able to live in wholeness so that you can enjoy life with a sense of peace and fulfillment. Trust the Lord today that He is healing all areas of brokenness of heart in your life!

QUESTIONS ANSWERED

DECLARATION

TODAY we decree that you receive answers to important questions, concerns, and thoughts. We say that insights from heaven come upon you to bring clarity and understanding. We break the power of all confusion, bewilderment, and clutter within your mind. We declare that all sense of misunderstanding or delusion cannot enter any part of your being, and we break the power of every evil spirit of error in the Name of Jesus. We pray that the Lord's peace rests upon you regarding those questions which only heaven can reveal in God's timing, and that a renewed trust in the guidance of your heavenly Father prevails. We say that your joy abounds above any sense of despair and that you are overshadowed by the truth that the Lord is always working on your behalf and is fighting for you! Amen!

SCRIPTURE

*I will instruct you and teach you in the way you should go;
I will counsel you with my loving eye on you* (Psalm 32:8
NIV).

WORD OF ENCOURAGEMENT

No one likes to have questions that they don't have a clear
answer for. Often we want an analytical explanation for the
quandaries we face. We also tend to desire similar explana-
tions for times when things didn't work out as we hoped.
However, not all questions can be answered this way. Sometimes God protects us from the details because we couldn't
handle them emotionally. Instead, He lays out truth for us by
providing inner peace regarding what we do not understand
and guidance that we cannot always see. What we can trust is
that God will never allow you to live in a place of perplexity without Him placing an assurance in your heart that
surpasses human understanding. In this way, He will
always provide clarity to the deepest questions and
concerns of your heart!

RISE UP AS AN OVERCOMER!

DECLARATION

TODAY we decree that you live as an overcomer and that defeat can never have a hold over you. We break the power of any cloud of failure that might exist over you and we say it is replaced by overwhelming success. We declare you are well able to rise above difficulty and struggle coming against your mind, body, family, occupation, and finances. We speak that you operate in the strength of the Lord and power of His might. We say what you put your hand to shall prosper. You are the head and not the tail, are above and not beneath, and no weapon formed against you shall prosper. We declare that you rise up today, that you overcome and stand strong in the power and grace of God upon you! Amen!

SCRIPTURE

Now thanks be unto God, which always causeth us to triumph in Christ, and maketh manifest the savour of his knowledge by us in every place (2 Corinthians 2:14).

WORD OF ENCOURAGEMENT

Having moments of failure in life is normal, but feeling continually like a failure isn't. However, it's not uncommon for people to live under an ongoing sense of failure or even experience seasons when it seems as if they cannot rise above the constant sense of defeat. Living under the cloud of constant failure is an evil spirit from the enemy and leads to things like depression and hopelessness. God wants to tear back the dark cloud of failure from your life and replace it with the triumph that Jesus Christ has already provided you. While life isn't perfect, it's still God's promise that we are able to experience a life that is marked by success. You are not a failure; you are an overcomer, and the Lord wants you to rise up in faith in this powerful truth today!

DEDICATION RENEWED;
CONDEMNATION BROKEN

DECLARATION

TODAY we decree that all areas of struggle, sin, iniquity, offense, and every generational curse is broken from your life. We say all negative or poor habits are removed and that a renewed consecration to the Lord rests upon you. We pray you have the strengthened faith to release all areas of weakness, failure, and feebleness before the foot of the cross. May you walk in the vast measure of liberty and forgiveness in Christ Jesus. We bind every spirit of the enemy from bringing condemnation, guilt, or shame, and we decree that you receive a full cleansing by the Word of God upon your entire being—spirit, soul, and body. May all worldly and earthly burdens be removed and may you take upon you the light and easy burden of Christ. May you live in a renewed and refreshed life of holiness and dedication to Jesus, and may your joy be both restored and made full in Him! Amen!

SCRIPTURE

There is therefore now no condemnation to them which are in Christ Jesus, who walk not after the flesh, but after the Spirit (Romans 8:1).

WORD OF ENCOURAGEMENT

Making a fresh commitment to the Lord is something that should be a part of every believer's life. Perhaps you have had certain areas that have not been fully surrendered to the Lord or perhaps have had seasons of not pressing in to Him as you should. Maybe you have allowed a sin area to have a place in your life. If there has been any kind of gap between you and the Lord, it can be repaired through repentance and by making a fresh commitment today. A habit of renewal and evaluation in our walk with God will keep us close to Him, and when we do so the curse of condemnation must be broken!

DECLARING SAME-DAY MIRACLES!

DECLARATION

TODAY we decree that you receive sudden answers to prayer. We declare that same-day miracles rest upon you. We say that you enter the season when things that have taken years and months will immediately manifest on the same day you pray! We prophesy that you receive your daily bread on *this* day! We break the power of every hindrance and blockage from the enemy in Jesus' Name! We bind the power of every attack that would come to defeat your faith and confidence. We bind weariness of mind and we loose hope and renewed zeal. We say the season of open doors, successes, blessings, favor, manifestation, opportunity, and increase rests upon you! We declare an end to decrease and we call for same-day miracles and immediate answers to prayer to break forth on every side right now! Amen!

SCRIPTURE

Give us this day our daily bread (Matthew 6:11).

WORD OF ENCOURAGEMENT

One of the key things Jesus demonstrated while on earth was the manifestation of immediate miracles and answers to prayer. He taught us to expect our daily bread on the same day we pray for it. Whenever people reached out to Him for help, He provided for their specific need instantly. Jesus said to the centurion, "As thou hast believed, so be it done unto thee" (Matt. 8:13), and the result was an immediate miracle for his servant. While there are waiting periods for certain things, God doesn't want us suffering while waiting for our essential needs. Begin the regular habit of trusting God that needless delay will be broken and immediate miracles and answers to prayer will happen on *this day*—the *same day* you pray!

A DOUBLE PORTION ANOINTING!

DECLARATION

TODAY we decree a double portion anointing of God's power to be upon you. According to Isaiah 61:7, we speak that you have a double portion anointing that replaces your season of shame. We say you receive a doubling of the anointing to prophesy, preach, declare, and pray. We say a tangible double anointing comes upon you to be a witness and to minister the Gospel to others. We pray that you receive a double portion anointing to pray for the sick, cast out evil spirits, and to walk in signs and wonders. We rebuke all intimidation and say that you stand bold and strong in your authority against the enemy and we decree that your season to shine has come! Right now, we call for a doubling upon the work of your hands to live in success and in God's divine blessing. We say that the level of power and blessing you have walked in up to this point accelerates and doubles immediately! Today we declare double, double, double to rest mightily and powerfully upon you! Amen!

SCRIPTURE

Instead of your shame you will receive a double portion, and instead of disgrace you will rejoice in your inheritance. And so you will inherit a double portion in your land, and everlasting joy will be yours (Isaiah 61:7 NIV).

WORD OF ENCOURAGEMENT

Most of us can immediately think of how our lives would change for the better if the good that we already have would double immediately. What we need to have confidence in is the fact that God wants us to always expect increase. Whether it's our ability to function in the gifts of the Spirit or that which pertains to natural provision, God wants His children blessed. Perhaps you have experienced a season when it seems things have decreased around you, but God is saying right now it's time to change that mindset and declare, "Double!"

A WORD IN
YOUR MOUTH

DECLARATION

TODAY we decree your mouth is filled with divine words. May you be released to declare, prophesy, pray, bind, loose, and sing new songs. Right now we declare that a watch is placed upon your tongue and that you will not speak anything contrary to the Word of the Lord or His promises and statutes. We say that your words are divinely inspired to bless others and that you have a mouth filled with wisdom. May your words also be filled with grace, seasoned with salt so that you know how to give an answer to every person who asks about the hope of the Gospel within you! We say right now in Jesus' Name that you know how to answer hard questions and that you speak with the power and authority of God upon you! We say your words have power and that there is a heavenly word in your mouth! Amen!

SCRIPTURE

Let your speech be always with grace, seasoned with salt, that ye may know how ye ought to answer every man (Colossians 4:6).

WORD OF ENCOURAGEMENT

Knowing what to say and having the right words for others, especially when they ask hard questions, isn't always easy from a natural perspective. We can sometimes feel concerned about what to say or how to give a proper biblical perspective. What we can have confidence in is knowing that the Holy Spirit within will fill our mouth whenever we need to speak for the Lord (see Luke 12:12). This means we can rely on a special anointing that teaches us what to say and how to say it when a situation arises. If we practice ensuring that we choose our words carefully and use them for God's purposes, then we can trust that He will give us what to say in every situation!

MIGHTY WARRIOR
ARISE!

DECLARATION

TODAY we decree that you rise up as a mighty warrior of the Spirit like Gideon. We speak a spirit of valor upon you right now! We declare you will not back down from the operations of the enemy that would work to intimidate, manipulate, or control you. We say that you are well equipped to wage war with the weapons of might that will pull down strongholds. We prophesy that you are rooted and grounded in love and that you shall never stumble or become offended by any fiery darts of the wicked. We declare that your faith will not fail. May you be surrounded with assurance and confidence that God is with you and He shall not allow you to fall or be defeated! We say it's so in Jesus' Name!

SCRIPTURE

And the angel of the Lord appeared unto him, and said unto him, The Lord is with thee, thou mighty man of valour (Judges 6:12).

WORD OF ENCOURAGEMENT

If you recall the story of Gideon for a moment, he was in a time when he was seeing the dire circumstances all around him and wondered why God let so many bad things happen. Yet the angel that appeared to him did not acknowledge Gideon's perspective. He simply told Gideon to rise up as a man of valor and take action. Gideon still struggled to see himself with the ability to do anything, but ended up being the very person used to deliver Israel. Sometimes we see our abilities as limited and don't feel we can rise from the daunting challenges surrounding us, but God wants you to see yourself today as the warrior He has made you! Changes begin when we look inside, and despite the current circumstances we grit our teeth and declare, "Rise up mighty warrior!"

YOUR EYES
ARE OPEN

DECLARATION

TODAY we decree your eyes are open to see what heaven is saying and doing in this important season. We pray that you are filled right now with spiritual wisdom, insight, and understanding. We declare that all spiritual blindness, confusion, deception, and darkness dissipate and that your heart and mind are flooded with light. We prophesy that you have an understanding like the tribe of Issachar to discern the times and seasons. We declare that any ungodly ideologies of the world will not infiltrate or control your beliefs, attitudes, and choices. We break the power of every ungodly soul tie and every lie from the enemy that is preventing you from gaining a righteous perspective. We say today that truth, divine revelation, and perception permeate your being and that nothing shall be able to enter your eye gate that is not from God! We place a boundary around your eyes, ears, and thoughts, and we say today that your eyes are open to see clearly according to the Spirit of the Lord! Amen!

SCRIPTURE

That the God of our Lord Jesus Christ, the Father of glory, may give unto you the spirit of wisdom and revelation in the knowledge of him: the eyes of your understanding being enlightened; that ye may know what is the hope of his calling, and what the riches of the glory of his inheritance in the saints (Ephesians 1:17-18).

WORD OF ENCOURAGEMENT

Being able to understand and know God's heart, mind, and plans is one of our greatest desires as believers. It also something God has made available to His children. Having this key ability to see heaven's perspective for our lives, circumstances, and even our cities and nations is something we should actively declare and pray for. It's the enemy who would want to keep us in the dark, but God will always shed His light and cause our eyes to be open!

DECLARING WHOLENESS

DECLARATION

TODAY we are declaring wholeness upon you—
spirit, soul, and body. We say that you receive a fresh
spiritual impartation from the throne room of heaven.
We say that revelation and insight comes to enlighten your
eyes in the things of the Spirit. We prophesy that your soul
is renewed and that your mind, will, emotions, intellect, and
memory are touched afresh by the anointing. All mind-binding and invasive demons that would try to control your
thoughts are bound and removed from torturing your thinking in the mighty Name of Jesus. We also speak and say that
your body receives a divine and tangible touch right now. All
pain, disease, infirmity, and chronic health issues are resolved
and healed by the power of God because of the stripes of Jesus
our Lord and Savior. We decree today that your entire person
is made whole from all that is not right and that you are new
and renewed in every part of your being!

SCRIPTURE

Thy faith hath made thee whole; go in peace, and be whole of thy plague (Mark 5:34).

WORD OF ENCOURAGEMENT

One of the key areas of life that we need to regularly exercise our faith for is to live in physical and emotional wholeness. This is God's desire for His people. In fact, Jesus paid for us to live a whole and abundant life (see Isa. 53:4-5; John 10:10). However, when we read many accounts of Jesus healing people, it wasn't enough for His healing power to be available to them. It required them connecting their faith and assurance with that healing power. Today as you decree over your life, know that consistent faith in God's promises will bring the things that have been broken in your life into a place to complete wholeness. Your faith has made you whole!

YOUR SEASON OF
EXPANSION AND ADVANCEMENT!

DECLARATION

WE decree today that you are loosed from a spirit of decay and decline. In the Name of Jesus we break all wicked operations by the princes and powers of the air and rulers of darkness and we say they are cast out from working against you! We decree that reduction is replaced with increase and enlargement. Decline is replaced with improvement, growth, and fruitfulness. Dead dreams are replaced with living, resurrected vision. We prophesy that your sense of purpose is refreshed once again! And, we say that all that has seemed to crumble is rebuilt by God's miraculous hand of power. We declare you are flourishing and a new season of expansion and advancement is upon you!

SCRIPTURE

Enlarge the place of your tent, and let them stretch out the curtains of your habitations; spare not, lengthen your cords, and strengthen your stakes. For you shall spread out to the right hand and to the left, and your descendants shall inherit the nations and make the desolate cities to be inhabited (Isaiah 54:2-3 MEV).

WORD OF ENCOURAGEMENT

Everyone has gone through seasons when they have experienced a sense of limitation. They feel limited financially, limited in their influence and relationships, or perhaps limited in their goals. No one wants to live from year to year feeling as though things are not improving or expanding in their life. We all want to see breakthrough that brings us into a place of greater abundance. We want to go from decrease to increase! As you continually declare increase, expansion, and advancement, those words will enable you to see past life's limitations. Remember, anyone can see the negatives around them, but it takes an anointing to see past that and see the expansion of God before you. Declare and envision your season of advancement and expansion upon you right now!

GOD IS GRANTING YOU BOLDNESS

DECLARATION

TODAY we decree that a new level of boldness, confidence, and fierceness for the Word of God and heavenly truths comes upon you. We command all timidity, intimidation, shyness, and fear to depart from you in Jesus' Name! Every lying spirit that would back you into a corner is bound. We say you are bold and confident like a lion to stand up for what you know and you are bold and strong to stand up for Jesus Christ. We say that you are well able to stand in the evil day and that you shall stand steadfastly in the promises, truths, and commands of the Word of God amidst opposition. We say you shall remain firm in faith for all that heaven has provided and taught you. We declare what God has destined for you shall come to pass and that a fresh, new endowment of boldness and assurance shall rest upon you in this season! Amen!

SCRIPTURE

The wicked flee when no man pursues, but the righteous are bold as a lion (Proverbs 28:1 MEV).

WORD OF ENCOURAGEMENT

Standing up boldly for the Lord in today's culture isn't always as easy as it sounds. Sure, we all want to believe we are valiant under pressure, but truth is every person has backed down from intimidation in some form or at some point. This is why we need the Lord's supernatural boldness to rest upon us and is why Proverbs 28:1 says that the righteous are more bold than the wicked. This isn't because we just possess a stronger personality or confrontational nature. It's because the Lord will anoint us with a special divine boldness that enables us to declare truth when it seems we are being pushed into a corner. May the Lord's divine boldness rest upon you today in a tangible way that enables you to speak what is pure and righteous amidst that which is wrong.

FIRE AND
PASSION IGNITED

DECLARATION

TODAY we decree that your fire and passion are ignited afresh. We declare that the flame of your first love in Christ is rekindled anew. We say that all lethargy is dispersed in Jesus' Name! We declare you receive a fresh baptism of the Holy Spirit and power. May your prayer language be as ignited as the first time you prayed in the Spirit. We speak that you are used in the gifts of the Spirit to lay hands upon the sick and they shall recover. We say the prophetic revelation gifts flow through you. May the gifts of power to cast out devils operate freely, and we say that you are ignited to be used by God in a new way in this season. May souls whom you come in contact with respond to the sound of your voice, and we prophesy that the word of God flowing through you shall not return void!

SCRIPTURE

Then His word was in my heart as a burning fire shut up in my bones (Jeremiah 20:9 MEV).

WORD OF ENCOURAGEMENT

Undoubtedly, like many others, your heart's desire is to be used by God in a supernatural way. There is no greater feeling than to carry God's supernatural faculties upon your life. It's a joyous experience to minister to the hurting or the sick or speak for God and see someone's life impacted. The wonderful thing is God wants us to operate in the supernatural gifts of the Spirit, and we can't allow ourselves to become discouraged or lethargic about functioning in this capacity. If you want to be used by the Lord at a greater level, it begins with passionate desire. Paul taught the church to desire the best gifts (see 1 Cor. 12:31). Along with such desire, by continually praying in the spirit and calling daily for the power of God to rest tangibly upon you, you will experience a growing passion for it and you will see Him manifest through you!

PURPOSE AND DESTINY REVIVED

DECLARATION

TODAY we decree that you see your destiny and calling through the eyes of the Spirit. We say that you see your purpose with faith. We declare that all clouded vision and blindness that would try to prevent you from seeing your bright future are destroyed in Jesus' Name. We prophesy that your barren season becomes fruitful. We declare that everything you are called to accomplish shall become manifest and that every prophetic word from heaven shall bear fruit. We command all gloominess to clear and we say bright days are before you.

SCRIPTURE

For I know the plans that I have for you, says the Lord, plans for peace and not for evil, to give you a future and a hope (Jeremiah 29:11 MEV).

WORD OF ENCOURAGEMENT

One of the key things the enemy uses to discourage believers is a loss of purpose when the circumstances around them paint a negative picture. Additionally, we each deeply want to know what we are called by God to be doing with the specific gifts and unique talents we have. There are three important factors to know when it comes to your calling, purpose, and destiny. First, if God planned it for you, it will happen, so don't allow the enemy's discouragement to dissuade you. Second, know that God gave you unique gifts and talents, and the thing you are destined to do will typically surround those talents. Be yourself and don't try to become something you aren't. God will enable you to do what you love and are good at doing. Last, remember God's timing. We typically want things on our timeframe, but there are many factors involved and God knows them all so we need to trust Him to work out the timing. Be strengthened today in the assurance that God has a good plan for your life and a future filled with hope!

FREE FROM DISCOURAGEMENT

DECLARATION

TODAY we decree that you are loosed from all discouragement. We break the power of every evil spirit of dismay, depression, and disappointment in the authority of Jesus' Name! We declare discouragement is replaced by great encouragement and that good news shall arrive. May the Holy Spirit of comfort and peace fill your soul. We say that your eyes see past the dark clouds and that you see the plan, purpose, and presence of God upon you and around you. We decree you are able to see a good outcome. We declare that no weapon formed against you shall prosper and every tongue that would rise up to accuse you shall be silenced by the power of God. Today, we say that a fresh anointing comes upon you and that your joy is restored to the fullest measure!

SCRIPTURE

Cast your burden on the Lord, and He will sustain you; He will never allow the righteous to be moved (Psalm 55:22 MEV).

WORLD OF ENCOURAGEMENT

Experiencing moments of temporary discouragement happens to all of us, but it's what we choose to do with that discouragement that determines the outcome. Discouragement is to be deprived of the hope that something is going to turn out alright. When Jesus' disciples were in the boat in a storm (see Mark 4:35-40) they reacted not only in great fear, but they expressed a form of discouragement through the assumption that they were going to die. The disciples couldn't see that all was going to be fine. However, Jesus responded by saying, "How is it that you had no faith?" They allowed discouragement to take over their thinking. We have to resist moments of discouragement. If we don't, then those moments will grow until our life is governed by feeling discouraged. Stand up today and decree against any discouragement that has tried to invade your thoughts and know that it's going to turn out alright!

FRESH INSIGHT
AND DISCERNMENT

DECLARATION

TODAY we decree you are filled with a fresh insight to all that the Spirit is speaking in this hour. May heaven's discernment and insight rest upon you. May your spiritual eyes and ears be anointed with fresh oil right now. We declare you will never be thwarted, deceived, or drawn off course by the entrapment of the enemy being laid out in this present hour. We break the power of every lying spirit of deception trying the ensnare God's elect and we say that you shall see clearly in this season and know what heaven is saying. We say you experience visions, dreams, insights, and encounters from the Throne. We say angelic movement occurs about you and that you are positioned to be one of God's agents to decree, declare, and operate in the Spirit for this end time season. We declare *nothing* shall pull you off course or blind you from the truth and all that you are called to do shall be fulfilled in the authority of Jesus' Name!

SCRIPTURE

But solid food belongs to those who are mature, for those who through practice have powers of discernment that are trained to distinguish good from evil (Hebrews 5:14 MEV).

WORD OF ENCOURAGEMENT

One of the most important elements believers must possess in this hour is discernment. Discernment is simply the ability to separate good from evil, right from wrong. It isn't being suspicious, nor does it carry a pious attitude toward others. A discerning believer is one who can stay on track and not become entangled in deception. So how do we become more discerning? We must feed on the Word of God and literally *practice* and train ourselves to look for where deception might be lurking. Sadly, many Christians do this to others' lives but aren't as careful to do so with their own. If you practice a life of discernment, it will enable you to be more precise and accurate with heavenly insight and in how to you speak for the Lord. Ask the Lord to help you become a more discerning Christian today!

BLESSINGS UPON
YOUR HOUSE

DECLARATION

TODAY we decree household blessings and salvations. We declare the visitation of God is coming to your house to release household blessings. We pray every member of your family shall be touched by the power and presence of God in a divine way. We break the power of every hindering spirit from coming against your home, family, property, and belongings in the Name of Jesus. We say that all works of darkness are bound. We speak an overshadowing of the Lord over your home and pray that angelic forces shall be released to protect and stand watch. We pray a new day over your home and that in this season every family member in your home comes into a new and fresh encounter with the Lord Himself!

SCRIPTURE

Believe in the Lord Jesus and you will be saved, along with everyone in your household (Acts 16:31 NLT).

WORD OF ENCOURAGEMENT

One of the dearest things on any believer's heart is the spiritual condition and wellbeing of their family members. The Bible has a considerable amount to say regarding the blessing of God coming upon households because one righteous person in the home or bloodline dared to believe for God's blessing upon their family. We see this in the life of the great patriarchs of Scripture and how God overshadowed their families and blessed their offspring because they prayed and asked God for it. It shows us that God cares about our loved ones and that His will is for whole families to come to Him. Not only should we make it a priority to pray and believe for a divine touch upon our family members, but we must have faith that God wants to touch them and is very willing to do so. God not only wants your lost loved ones to be saved, but He wants to place His hand of blessing upon every member of your family! Declare a household blessing upon your family members and believe today that all your house shall be saved!

MARKED
FOR FAVOR!

DECLARATION

TODAY we decree supernatural favor over you! What God favors, He empowers; so we declare you are empowered for increase, esteem, and blessing. May every unfavorable, wrongful "no" be turned into a "yes" so you will not be passed over or denied. We say that closed doors are replaced by new open doors and that this day you shall encounter favorable responses and respect from those you meet and interact with. We say every enemy that has come against you will come to peace and all hostile attacks, accusations, and false rumors against you will cease. We prophesy benefits and divine surprises, new opportunities, and invitations. May you be welcomed, celebrated, and honored. This day we declare you are marked for favor!

SCRIPTURE

For thou, Lord, wilt bless the righteous; with favour wilt thou compass him as with a shield (Psalm 5:12).

WORD OF ENCOURAGEMENT

There are few things that boost one's confidence like the feeling of being appreciated, accepted, and at times celebrated. No one likes the feeling of trying to accomplish something only to encounter closed doors and denials. We want to experience favor, but the good news is that we as believers already have favor with God! When we live for God, seek Him, and strive to do His will, God's promise is that He will surround our life with favor. That means He will set you up in the right circumstances and put the right people in your path who will grant you a place of appreciation and celebration. When you are favored, doors are opened that you can't always explain, blessings come that surprise you, and often people who were against you suddenly change their position. Believe God as you make your declaration today that you are surrounded with a mighty shield and that you are marked for favor!

DECLARE A
NEW SEASON

DECLARATION

TODAY we decree you are divinely transferred into a new and glorious season from the Lord. We command all the cycles of trouble, hindrance, warfare, and disappointment to cease in Jesus' Name. We say a new prophetic declaration is being written over you that places you in a season of peace, prosperity, blessing, and restfulness. We bind the works of darkness from filling your mind with fear and resentment. We break the power of all lethargy and apprehension that arose from the circumstances surrounding the former season and we say you are infused with new seeds of fresh fire, vision, excitement, and faith for what is ahead. We say you are advancing into greater days and that your joy shall be made full! It's your time to shine because a new and brighter season is upon you.

SCRIPTURE

Remember ye not the former things, neither consider the things of old. Behold, I will do a new thing; now it shall spring forth; shall ye not know it? I will even make a way in the wilderness, and rivers in the desert (Isaiah 43:18-19).

WORD OF ENCOURAGEMENT

We understand that seasons come and go in our lives and that some seasons are better than others. There are seasons that are filled with great challenge, and sometimes when you have faced such times it's easy to dwell on them emotionally. Often it's because the old season left a scar in our soul and a negative imprint on our memory. If it was an extremely difficult time, the thoughts and memories often try to continually resurface. It's important to know that Jesus came to heal the brokenhearted and was also chastised so we could live our lives filled with peace (see Luke 4:18; Isa. 53:4-5). Jesus provided a way so you could be delivered emotionally from the past season and be able to wholly embrace what is emerging. Declare your new season today, knowing that the former season is fading away and something new is here!

DECREE OVER YOUR
OCCUPATION AND BUSINESS

DECLARATION

TODAY we decree over you regarding your job, business, and occupation. We are asking the Lord to set up divine connections, interactions, events, appointments, and God-encounters. May you be able to interact with people of influence to help set you up for success. We declare open doors, interviews, contacts, contracts, new clients, and customers. We speak that raises, bonuses, tips, and commissions will come into your hands speedily. We declare promotions and awards for a job well done. We prophesy favor when you come in and when you go out. We declare you receive fresh ideas that create acceleration and advancement. We say that you will not be ignored, declined, passed over, or left out in Jesus' Name because you are the head and not the tail, above only and not below. Today we say that you are gainfully and steadily employed and that success and blessing shall be your portion!

SCRIPTURE

The Lord will send a blessing on your barns and on everything you put your hand to. The Lord your God will bless you in the land he is giving you (Deuteronomy 28:8 NIV).

WORD OF ENCOURAGEMENT

The first few verses of Deuteronomy 28 are promises that were written to Israel under the law of Moses reminding the people that if they would serve God wholeheartedly, in return God would ensure blessing on all aspects of their lives. We often refer to these verses as the blessing of the covenant, and if you notice, a great deal of it relates to a person's work life. It speaks of having success in business, financial surplus, and blessing on one's property and assets. These promises are reiterated in various ways throughout Scripture—if you serve God, He will bless your occupational endeavors. The Lord wants you to take hold of that truth in your spirit today so you can begin to wake up each morning expecting your work life to be productive, successful, and blessed!

BINDING UP
WEARINESS

DECLARATION

TODAY we break the power of all weariness in Jesus' Name! We say that every evil entity from the enemy is rendered powerless to steal your resolve and rob you of your determination. We call upon the heavenly hosts to be released and wage war on your behalf. We pray the Lord supplies you with supernatural strength so that you can stand your ground. You will mount up with eagle's wings, run and not grow weary, you will walk and not faint, and we say you are completely overshadowed with faith and power! You shall not become tired in well doing. You will stay the course and finish all that heaven has given you to do without giving up or giving in to pressure. We declare your harvest shall not be stolen from you in Jesus' Name!

SCRIPTURE

Let us not become weary in doing good, for at the proper time we will reap a harvest if we do not give up (Galatians 6:9 NIV).

WORD OF ENCOURAGEMENT

There are many things in our modern life that create pressure and come to discourage our faith. It can range from everyday challenges to direct persecution for our faith and beliefs or everything in between. The enemy's goal is to get us to stop believing, stop standing up for what we believe, and to ultimately change course. He doesn't want you to keep standing firm on God's promises, His principles, or His truths. Often if the pressure to quit is strong enough, we are in a place where we could easily shift our stance and stop believing or stop standing up for what is right. One thing that will keep us from doing that is to simply declare that we won't do it! Speak and prophesy today that you will not grow weary and give up. Declare that you will stay the course in whatever area that you are standing in faith about and that you will stand to the finish until you reap your harvest in full!

UNDOING HEAVY BURDENS!

DECLARATION

RIGHT now, we decree that you are released and free from every heavy burden that is trying to weigh you down. We say that you receive the light and easy yoke of Christ that enables you to rise up and live in wholeness, freedom, peace, and joy. In the Name of Jesus we bind up every lie of the enemy that would make you believe that you will never come out from under the weight of affliction! We command all demonic oppression to come off of you. We say that according to Nahum 1:9, your season of affliction must end and it shall not rise a second time and whom the Son sets free is free indeed. We declare relief, alleviation, and deliverance from the burden created by the demands of life. We speak this over you and say it manifests and rests upon you now!

SCRIPTURE

Then Jesus said, "Come to me, all of you who are weary and carry heavy burdens, and I will give you rest. Take my yoke upon you. Let me teach you, because I am humble and gentle at heart, and you will find rest for your souls. For my yoke is easy to bear, and the burden I give you is light" (Matthew 11:28-30 NLT).

WORD OF ENCOURAGEMENT

When Jesus spoke about us taking His "yoke" upon us, He was using a term that refers to a harness worn by a set of oxen or plowing animals. He was emphasizing that the pressures and demands of this life can tether us to an unseen harness of sorts that causes us to live every day feeling as if we are just plowing through rather than living. It's like the old saying "surviving not thriving." What Jesus was saying is that when we live our lives in such a way that we are "harnessed" to or focused on Him, rather than just immersed in all the pressures of this life, we will find that the heavy burdens life can pile upon us are alleviated. Focus today on the Lord's ability to alleviate those pressures and declare that you are free from every feeling of being burdened down!

INVADING FEAR
MUST GO!

DECLARATION

TODAY we *decree* that any form of fear trying to invade your life is bound up in the Name of Jesus! We come against all financial fear and say that every monetary need is met this year. We bind all fear regarding your family and loved ones. We say they are protected by God's angelic hosts. We decree that all fear of death and tragedy is bound and destroyed! We bind the fear of sickness and disease. We say that every fear of failure, rejection, oppression, and depression must leave you right now! We break off all fear of the future concerning the nations and world events and we declare these things shall have no ability to torment your mind. You are favored and blessed of God and *all* shall be well concerning you! We agree on this together in faith, in Jesus' mighty Name!

SCRIPTURE

Don't be afraid, for I am with you. Don't be discouraged, for I am your God. I will strengthen you and help you. I will hold you up with my victorious right hand (Isaiah 41:10 NLT).

WORD OF ENCOURAGEMENT

Fear in the lives of people is a very real and demonic entity. Satan loves to capitalize on the types of things that create fear in a person's mind. He wants us to envision the possibility of tragedy, failure, sickness, and the like. He will use events from things like a news story, a friend's experience, or perhaps something that happened to you personally. He then uses these to implant an image inside of us that something will go terribly wrong and with it attempt to make us believe that God will not rescue us from it. We have the choice to not let the spirit of fear or the imagination of fearful events invade our thoughts. We can overcome the enemy's tactic of fear by speaking the opposite. We can command fearful thoughts to leave us. Our words of faith will enable us to shift our mental images onto the fact that God's great and miraculous hand is working for us in every situation and that there is no reason to fear!

BINDING UP
TROUBLING SPIRITS

DECLARATION

WE declare this shall be a day filled with God's grace, blessings, goodness, and mercy. We bind all harassing and troubling works of the enemy in Jesus' Name and say that all frustration, bad news, disappointment, letdown, discouragement, aggravation, and disturbances have no place in your day. We prophesy that you will not have to hassle with annoying moments that steal from the joy of the day and meddle with your plans and schedule. Angelic forces are being released so that you are protected and nothing shall harm or injure you. We take authority over evil spirits that would cause family troubles and strife, breakdowns and setback, and we say this will be a day filled with peace, fun, and joy! All shall be well this day, this week, month, and year! We speak it in Jesus' Name! Amen!

SCRIPTURE

Then the people of the land weakened the hands of the people of Judah, and troubled them in building (Ezra 4:4).

WORD OF ENCOURAGEMENT

When the people of God set out to rebuild the temple in the book of Ezra they encountered a continual onslaught of harassments. The Bible says those who were in disagreement with their efforts "troubled them in building." In other words, they created little problems here and there to try and make them feel frustrated. In a similar way we can experience little troubles, often created by the enemy that can make us feel like we are always addressing some little problem. God wants you to enjoy days of peace and order, not putting out fires, constantly fixing something, and running around in panic and stress. Speak to any harassing spirits that might try and discourage you and make you feel like you are always stressed out. Declare that troubling spirits cannot interfere in your day!

HOPE RESTORED!

DECLARATION

TODAY we decree that your hope is restored and springs forth as a tree of life. We say that every delay is converted into acceleration. We prophesy that every setback becomes a setup for something greater than you dreamed. We break the spirit of delay and say you receive a new sense of anticipation and confidence. We pray that blessings, increase, and fullness will break loose and overflow upon you for this current season. We speak to your future and destiny and declare that all God has planned for you cannot be aborted by the enemy in Jesus' Name and good things will begin to manifest before you! It's a season of good. Take it, it's yours!

SCRIPTURE

Hope deferred maketh the heart sick: but when the desire cometh, it is a tree of life (Proverbs 13:12).

WORD OF ENCOURAGEMENT

Losing hope is a serious thing because hope is what creates our vision. It's the picture in our mind that we can set our faith and efforts upon. Without vision people perish (see Prov. 29:18). It takes vision to accomplish anything. However, when difficulty is constant enough, people tend to lose that hope and vision if they don't defend themselves against this tendency. You know your hope has been compromised when you can't see your heart's desire ever coming to fruition. Hopelessness is not from God and is something we need to recognize and resist. Even though it may seem like everything is against you, stand up with fresh ambition and resist that feeling. Ask the Lord to restore your hope and help you see your future through His eyes! Let's declare that your hope is restored today.

PROPHETIC INSIGHT

DECLARATION

TODAY we declare you receive wisdom and prophetic insight for everything you do today and for every decision you must make. We say your spiritual ears are open to what heaven is saying to you with pinpoint accuracy. May the heart, mind, and intent of God be downloaded into your spirit. May you experience prophetic visions and dreams. We prophesy that you hear the secrets of God. We break off any deaf and dumb spirits that would come to disrupt your spiritual hearing and knowing. We declare you will not receive, hear, or communicate anything that is not of God. We break the power of confusion and misinformation from coming against your mind and declare all voices not from God cannot interfere. We speak now that your prophetic spirit is alive and active to know what is of God and that you are able to speak for Him with precision in Jesus' Name!

SCRIPTURE

The eyes of your understanding being enlightened; that ye may know what is the hope of his calling, and what the riches of the glory of his inheritance in the saints (Ephesians 1:18).

WORD OF ENCOURAGEMENT

As Spirit-filled believers, we are prophetic people. We carry within us the person of the Holy Spirit who talks to us and imparts to us the heart, mind, and intentions of God. He wants to speak to us not just regarding our own lives, but also for others in our lives and even regarding things happening in the world. This is why the Bible says in the last days, God would pour out His Spirit on all flesh and that we would prophesy and experience visions and dreams (see Acts 2:17-18). First Corinthians 12 shows us that the gifts of the Spirit should be active in the church. God wants the prophetic anointing flowing through His people! At the same time, we want to be accurate and disciplined to hear prophetic secrets. Declare today the prophetic insight will rest upon you in a mighty way!

JOY IN KNOWING HIM!

DECLARATION

TODAY we declare that you experience the renewed joy of knowing Jesus. May you know Him and the power of His resurrection. May you know and receive His great love. We declare you have revelation of His tangible anointing upon you. We pray you have revelation knowledge in Him that provides you wisdom, direction, and understanding. We pray that you experience a fresh excitement about spiritual things. May your divine knowledge of the Lord enable you to have assurance of His faithfulness and grace resting over your life. We declare right now that every spirit of fear and confusion is bound, and we say that your awareness of the Lord's presence takes precedence in your thoughts. We declare you sense God upon you and around you all day in Jesus' glorious Name!

SCRIPTURE

Restore unto me the joy of thy salvation (Psalm 51:12).

WORD OF ENCOURAGEMENT

If you have served God and been a Christian for any length of time, you can fall into the trap of familiarity with your own salvation. Of course no one intentionally does this, but in the daily grind of our schedules, the repetition of church attendance, we can make our walk with God a formula or routine without even knowing it and take our salvation for granted. It's important to recall the moment you were first saved and gave your heart to the Lord. Think back to when you were first filled with the Spirit and the excitement that filled your soul! This is what David was saying when he asked the Lord to restore the joy of his salvation. In David's case, he had fallen into sin, but undoubtedly that process began by him becoming familiar with his salvation in some way or another and perhaps even taking it for granted. Ask the Lord for and declare that a renewed joy in knowing Him comes upon you!

ANOINTED
AND APPOINTED!

DECLARATION

TODAY we decree over you that you are called by God. You are anointed and appointed for a divine purpose to accomplish something fruitful and lasting. We prophesy a fresh anointing for heavenly service comes upon you. Like Jesus, we say you are empowered to go about doing good and setting people free from oppression. We declare you will impact lives in a divine way. We bind the works of the enemy to devalue you and try to pull you into lethargy or a place that is void of purpose. We say that your goals are defined and ordained from heaven and may all you set your hand to do prosper. May you accomplish more this year and do more for the Kingdom of God than ever before. Let divine doors be opened before you that will bring you before people of influence that you might affect them with the anointing. We declare it in Jesus' Name!

SCRIPTURE

How God anointed Jesus of Nazareth with the Holy Ghost and with power: who went about doing good, and healing all that were oppressed of the devil; for God was with him (Acts 10:38).

WORD OF ENCOURAGEMENT

Let's be honest and say that when we gave our lives to the Lord it was not just about us. Yes, it is about us knowing Him, but then we are called to share that with others. However, it's not enough to just share Jesus and our own personal testimony. We need to be able to demonstrate the anointing! We need to be able to help people experience the power of God and His miracles. Alongside that, we also need the Lord to set up divine doors and strategies for us to demonstrate His power. God wants to not only anoint you, but appoint you for His service in whatever circle of influence you have. Whether at your job or to your family and friends, we need to be anointed so that people don't just hear about Jesus, but they see His power and experience a change in their lives. Declare today you are anointed and appointed!

RESTORATION AND PAYBACK!

DECLARATION

TODAY we decree that you experience restoration from the years the locust and cankerworm have eaten. May everything that has seemed to have decayed or crumbled be reestablished into newness, and may you begin to flourish again. In the Spirit, we prophesy a rebuilding of the old waste places and that streams begin to flow in the desert. We break the power of destruction, attack, and devastation in Jesus' Name. We pray that you begin to receive restitution, payback, benefits, and reimbursements. We pray that fruitfulness will remain in your life and that you will experience fulfillment, success, and complete contentment. We ask that all that God has planned for your life will begin to fully manifest in this season before you! We speak all of this in Jesus' Name.

SCRIPTURE

And I will restore to you the years that the locust hath eaten, the cankerworm, and the caterpiller, and the palmerworm, my great army which I sent among you. And ye shall eat in plenty, and be satisfied, and praise the name of the Lord your God, that hath dealt wondrously with you: and my people shall never be ashamed (Joel 2:25-26).

WORD OF ENCOURAGEMENT

What is particularly significant about our verses here in Joel 2 is the fact that it speaks of a season of decrease and decay in terms of years, meaning it was a long, arduous season. Sometimes when there are areas that we have dealt with for a long time, such as an ongoing health issue, lengthy season of insufficient financial supply, or a drawn-out family struggle, we can fall into the repetitive cycle of that season until we can't see anything different. Often under such circumstances we can begin to tolerate what is, and not expect a time of restoration to ever emerge. It's time to expect that God will take that long season and restore everything that was lost during it. Change your expectation today and know that restoration and payback is upon you!

MENTAL OPPRESSION IS BOUND

DECLARATION

TODAY we decree you overcome all manner of fatigue that may be trying to set you back. We bind tiredness, physical exhaustion, mental oppression, and emotional stress. May the fear and distress of this world be far from you, and we bind all manner of doom, depression, and downheartedness in the Name of Jesus. We say anxiety has no place near you. We call for angels to surround you, and may the peace of the Holy Spirit give you the assurance that all is well and good things shall be your portion! We declare you experience calm, peace, and tranquility. We declare comfort, contentment, and complete relief in your mind that shall cause you to smile and rejoice. We decree all is well and shall be well! Amen!

SCRIPTURE

Looking unto Jesus the author and finisher of our faith; who for the joy that was set before him endured the cross, despising the shame, and is set down at the right hand of the throne of God. For consider him that endured such contradiction of sinners against himself, lest ye be wearied and faint in your minds (Hebrews 12:2-3).

WORD OF ENCOURAGEMENT

Emotions are powerful. They are wonderful because they allow us to feel joy and good feelings. Contrarily, they can also impact us with feelings of despair and make us believe things that aren't true. The enemy loves to capitalize on our negative emotions to discourage our faith and purpose. He uses such emotions to wear us down. If we don't deal with these emotions we can eventually become mentally oppressed, where we struggle to see any positive future. Thinking about Jesus and declaring His Name will help you overcome mental oppression. Consider today all that He endured to obtain victory on your behalf. When we think about Jesus in this way, we can't help but see a victorious outcome and mental oppression will have to flee!

DIVINE REVERSAL!

DECLARATION

TODAY we decree divine reversal! We say that discouragement turns into encouragement, setbacks become increase, fear becomes faith, and all lack turns into surplus. We declare that sickness becomes health and fatigue is replaced by energy and life. We declare that hindrances move out of the way and are replaced by breakthrough and results. We declare that every question becomes an answer and that all areas of confusion turn into clarity. We decree that strife becomes unity and frustration turns into success. We say all things that have been negatively set into motion are now completely reversed! May all that concerns you experience a complete and total divine reversal and turnaround from heaven in Jesus' mighty Name!

SCRIPTURE

The Lord shall cause thine enemies that rise up against thee to be smitten before thy face: they shall come out against thee one way, and flee before thee seven ways (Deuteronomy 28:7).

WORD OF ENCOURAGEMENT

Growing up, most of us learned in science class that when something has been set in motion, it will stay in motion until it is interrupted by an opposing force. This fact also holds true in spiritual things. For example, Proverbs 18:21 says we can set the power of death and life into motion by what we say. If we speak negatively, we set negative things (death) into motion. If we speak positively, we also put the positive (life) into motion. Whatever we have been speaking will stay in motion until it is interrupted by the opposite. Today we are releasing the opposite to any negatives that have been in motion in your life. The enemy may have come against you in some way, but we are releasing the opposite with our words of declaration and expecting a divine reversal to occur that sends the forces of darkness running in the opposite direction! Declare today that negatives in your life will be reversed in Jesus' Name!

CHALLENGING PLACES EASED

DECLARATION

TODAY we decree that the challenging places in your life become easier. We call upon the God who makes the crooked places straight and the rough places plain. We command every opposing mountain and hindrance to be removed in the Name of Jesus! We pray for God's guidance and assurance as you take the next steps before you and that you shall be surefooted as you go. We pray that you have a divine ability from God to make wise decisions with confidence. We pray for strength, energy, and renewed faith. May the Spirit of the Lord cause you to experience relief from that which has been difficult and hard to navigate and may you come into a season of rest! We decree this to be so in Jesus' mighty Name!

SCRIPTURE

Every valley shall be exalted, and every mountain and hill shall be made low: and the crooked shall be made straight, and the rough places plain (Isaiah 40:4).

WORD OF ENCOURAGEMENT

Most of us ask God for His divine wisdom in the decisions we make. We also couple that with our natural human wisdom that God gives us. Wisdom is an important key in navigating the course of life, and the Bible tells us it's the principle thing to have (see Prov. 4:7). However, in addition to wisdom we also sometimes need the circumstances around us to settle! We need things to smooth out so we aren't spending countless hours trying to navigate rough waters. We can call on the Lord and ask Him to smooth out the rough places before us so by the time we get there it will be smooth sailing. Psalm 23:2 says He will lead you beside still waters. That means He eases the challenges. Yes, challenges do come, but life isn't to be a constant battle with difficult things. Exercise your faith today for the path before you to be eased and challenges made smooth in Jesus' Name!

FRESH INSPIRATION AND VISION

DECLARATION

TODAY we decree that lost vision and purpose are restored. We pray that you receive refreshed inspiration concerning every project before you and for your future. May you see your God-given destiny with a renewed mindset. We declare that you become motivated to accomplish everything God has called you to do. We bind up the power of discouragement, lethargy, and indifference in Jesus' Name! We break every pattern and repetitive cycle of failure and say it will not continue. We speak new life to everything that has grown stale and fallen dormant. We decree your gifts and talents are stirred up afresh. We call for a supernatural wave of enthusiasm, passion, and determination to finish everything you have inside your heart from the Lord! You are called, anointed, and appointed for something amazing—for such a time as this!

SCRIPTURE

For the vision is yet for an appointed time, but at the end it shall speak, and not lie: though it tarry, wait for it; because it will surely come, it will not tarry (Habakkuk 2:3).

WORD OF ENCOURAGEMENT

When God drops something in our heart, it's because there is a purpose for it. It's something He intends to be carried out to completion. The enemy, however, is all about aborting what is meant to be completed. He wants our lives to be filled with a list of things that didn't come to fruition and remain incomplete or aborted altogether. Whether it's a ministry calling, business venture, a project, or even things like right relationships, the devil wants you to feel the sense of failure from incompletion. Every person must resist the urge to abandon what God has appointed during times when we aren't feeling as excited and enthusiastic. We must remind ourselves there is an appointed time for what we have begun to be completed. Keep your eyes on the appointed time of completion that God has already established and it will carry you through!

UNEXPECTED
BLESSINGS AND SURPRISES!

DECLARATION

TODAY we decree that you receive unexpected blessings, surprises, increases, and overflow. We prophesy that you shall be pleasantly surprised by good news and good reports. We declare that bad and unexpected news shall not interfere and disrupt your peace in Jesus' Name. We pray that good tidings shall break out on your right and left and it shall be as cool water that replenishes the dry places in your life. May you be divinely surprised by blessings you didn't even ask for, and we decree that good news begins to overtake all negative reports. We pray the Lord will send people in your path from many places who shall have something good to tell you. We say that you have all sufficiency in all things and your cup runs over. We pray that you will flourish abundantly and goodness and mercy will follow you wherever you go in Jesus' mighty Name!

SCRIPTURE

Finally hearing good news from a distant land is like a drink of cold water when you are dry and thirsty (Proverbs 25:25 GNT).

WORD OF ENCOURAGEMENT

There are few things that can add a bright spot in a person's day like getting a good report or some good news, especially news that you didn't expect. As we read in the verse above, there is something about getting good news that acts like water on a thirsty soul. It clears your mind and gives you a new sense of hope and determination. Everyone loves to hear good news! Yet, often even though there is good news around us, sometimes we miss it because negative news has overtaken our focus. Make a point to do two things today: 1) focus on the good news that *is* happening around you; 2) ask God for good news to come your way. In fact, it is an act of faith to pray for that. God doesn't want you living life bracing for the worst, but rather expecting the best. By asking Him to bring good tidings into your life, you are showing Him that you expect His best to be your life's experience. Expect good news and divine surprises!

NO WEAPON OF LIES CAN PROSPER!

DECLARATION

WE decree today that no weapon formed against you can prevail. Every weapon of wrongful accusation or indictment must bow to the Name of Jesus. Today, we declare you are able to put on the full armor of God that you may stand firm against the works of the evil one and rise above every word of judgement. We say any word or rumor unjustly uttered against you shall crumble and fail. We bind up every demonic assault against your character in Jesus' Name. You will not be overcome by losses, decreases, or setbacks from things said that are not true. We declare that every lie perpetrated by the forces of darkness is exposed and silenced. May your mind be clear from the enemy's whispers. We declare that your victory and freedom manifests speedily in Jesus' Name!

SCRIPTURE

No weapon that is formed against thee shall prosper; and every tongue that shall rise against thee in judgment thou shalt condemn. This is the heritage of the servants of the Lord, and their righteousness is of me, saith the Lord (Isaiah 54:17).

WORD OF ENCOURAGEMENT

There is an old saying: "don't borrow trouble," which essentially means *don't assume the worst*. One of the most common areas where we struggle with this is when we face trials and then feel pressed upon by lies, rumors, and what we *think* people are saying. Overcoming what you think might be getting said about you negatively is one of the greatest victories you can win. When the Bible tells us no weapon formed against you shall prosper, it says so in context of words spoken about you that come to condemn or damage your integrity. Believe today that God is big enough to handle the naysayers and slanderers and that you will be exonerated from their lies. We can spend so much of our time worrying about what someone is saying that we miss what God is saying. Trust today that no weapon formed against you can prosper!

STRENGTH
TO FORGIVE

DECLARATION

TODAY we declare that you receive the strength and ability to forgive every person who has hurt, betrayed, mistreated, and wronged you. May the overwhelming power of God's forgiveness rise up within. We decree that every painful memory is erased from your soul. May the burden of every offense and transgression committed against you be released from your shoulders. We prophesy that you are liberated from the stronghold of unforgiveness that would interfere with your prayers and rob your peace. We say that you are able to set aside the misdeeds of others and move forward into your bright future. We speak this and say you are able to freely say, "I forgive them in Jesus' Name!"

SCRIPTURE

And when ye stand praying, forgive, if ye have ought against any: that your Father also which is in heaven may forgive you your trespasses (Mark 11:25).

WORD OF ENCOURAGEMENT

One of the most vast subjects in Scripture is the topic of forgiveness, and our entire salvation is based on it. Jesus came to pay the penalty for our sins so we could be forgiven by God. This is why it is so important to forgive. Jesus taught that we can't expect to be forgiven by God when we can't forgive others (see Matt. 18:21-35). That said, sometimes it can be hard to get past the feelings of resentment regarding what others have done to us and to stop reliving the hurtful memories. This is where we ask God for the strength to forgive. It may be difficult in our own power, but forgiveness begins with acknowledging we must do so, and we can ask God to help us. Forgiving someone doesn't mean every relationship needs to be restored; in fact, certain relationships cannot be rebuilt for many reasons. What it does mean is that you aren't continuously thinking about vengeance or how they hurt you. Make the firm decision to release the wrongdoings of others from your mind and begin that today by simply declaring, "I forgive them!"

A KEEN
EAR TO HEAR

DECLARATION

WE decree that you have a keen ear to hear the voice, instruction, mind, and direction of the Holy Spirit. We say that you are able to know what the Spirit is saying in this important hour. We declare you carry an understanding of what heaven is doing and you know the times and seasons of God. We prophesy that you will never be confused or pulled off course by the man-made trends of the current culture. We break the power of confusion, manipulation, and peer pressure that would come to dissuade you from the call and purposes of the Holy Spirit. May you have a sharpened ear to know when the Spirit would interrupt your plans and intentions. We say that you are one who can interpret the strategies of God. We prophesy that you can hear the wind of the Spirit and know which way to follow in Jesus' Name.

SCRIPTURE

If any man have ears to hear, let him hear (Mark 4:23).

He that hath an ear, let him hear what the Spirit saith unto the churches (Revelation 2:11).

WORD OF ENCOURAGEMENT

We are living in a morally declining culture where godlessness is on the rise. More than ever, it's important to have an ear that can hear the direction and move of the Holy Spirit. Jesus said that deception would be rampant in the last days (see Matt. 24) and it would require us to be on the alert so we ourselves don't become misguided. But more than just becoming misguided, we must also be a people who can hear the Spirit's plans and purposes so we can know our heavenly assignments. We must have ears to hear His instructions so we can reach this culture with the Gospel. We are to be God's warriors of truth and it requires us to know His plans and directives. Ask the Lord to give you a spiritual ear to hear so that you will not be misguided by popular opinions and conceptions, but rather that which the Spirit is saying. Ask for a keen ear to hear!

JOY AND LAUGHTER

DECLARATION

TODAY we decree you receive joy unspeakable and fullness of glory! May laughter fill your heart and a smile flood your countenance. We take authority over every stronghold of grief, sorrow, depression, hopelessness, and anguish. We command every dark cloud over you to dissipate in the Name of Jesus. We declare your thoughts become filled with the light of God's goodness. We pray you receive a fresh sense of hope, confidence, faith, and purpose regarding your future. We prophesy that you experience gladness in your heart. We pray that you rise up in renewed faith that enables you to see that *everything* is going to be alright! We are asking God that you will receive good news today! Declare it's going to be a great day!

SCRIPTURE

A merry heart doeth good like a medicine: but a broken spirit drieth the bones (Proverbs 17:22).

WORD OF ENCOURAGEMENT

We probably have all heard of various scientific studies that talk about how smiles, joy, and laughter can affect one's health. Well, we have proof from Scripture that this is true! A merry or happy heart acts like medicine to the cells of our body. Our health is impacted by our level of gladness. However, challenging or painful circumstances can try to steal that sense of joyfulness. Instead of feeling elated, we feel a churning within. That is when we need to pray in faith for our sense of gladness to return and we can ask for God to do that by only a power He can provide. We can't always in our human strength muster up the ability to laugh and rejoice in tough times, but we can speak words of joy and ask God to bring supernatural joy upon us. If you aren't feeling much joy or the desire to laugh, ask the Father to invade you with a gladness that overrides everything that ails you. Declare joy and laughter today!

A DEEP
CLEANSING

DECLARATION

TODAY we declare that you shall experience a fresh cleansing from the Spirit of God. We prophesy a deep cleaning that clears your mind, changes your ideas, invades your heart, and draws you closer to the Lord. May the fuller's soap of heaven wash your life from all levels of contamination that would place a wedge between you and the Holy One. We decree right now a washing of the water of God's Word to clear from you all the debris of this world. May you be flooded with clean spiritual water that goes into the depths of your soul in Jesus' Name. We undo all the powers of the enemy that would contaminate, infiltrate, and degrade your spiritual purity and solidarity. Right now we speak that you are clean, renewed, and purified by the fire and power of the precious Holy Spirit!

SCRIPTURE

But who may abide the day of his coming? and who shall stand when he appeareth? for he is like a refiner's fire, and like fullers' soap (Malachi 3:2).

WORD OF ENCOURAGEMENT

Facing personal impurities can be a tough thing. No one enjoys looking at their own faults and failures. However, Scripture repeatedly reminds us of its importance. It's not to condemn us, but rather to better us. We all need to take the time to look within, but we also need to allow God to do the same. The Bible reveals the Lord is like a fire, which burns up impurities. He is also like the soap of one who does the laundry (fuller's soap). He is there to wash what needs to be removed. God isn't there to condemn our failings; instead, He comes to cleanse them so we can stand as pure vessels in the day of His return. He also comes to cleanse us so we can enjoy a clear conscience and sense of liberty from guilt. God wants to regularly do a deep cleansing in our lives, just like we do seasonal cleanings in our homes. Don't deny Him this powerful touch in your life. Ask the Father to enact a deep cleansing in your spirit, soul, and body today!

IMMEASURABLE PEACE

DECLARATION

TODAY we decree you receive immeasurable peace. We declare that you are surrounded by both external and internal peace that passes understanding and overrides thoughts of fear, doubt, worry, and anxiety. We speak to every area of nervousness and say that it is dissipated by the supernatural peace of God in Jesus' Name. We bind every storm that is trying to create chaos and steal your peace and we declare to those storms, "Peace, be still!" May your mind, will, and emotions come into soundness and wholeness regarding every circumstance in your life. We declare that your heart is filled with faith and assurance and we say that you will reach the other side of every difficult journey and you shall do so in victory! We decree it in Jesus' glorious Name!

SCRIPTURE

Be careful for nothing; but in every thing by prayer and supplication with thanksgiving let your requests be made known unto God. And the peace of God, which passeth all understanding, shall keep your hearts and minds through Christ Jesus (Philippians 4:6-7).

WORD OF ENCOURAGEMENT

Obviously, there are many things in this life that come to rob us of that sense of peace and tranquility we all crave. It can be anything from just a very busy schedule and family demands to the trials and storms of life. What we need to know is that it is *not* God's will for us to live in constant distress. Jesus said that He would give us His peace and therefore we should not allow our heart to be troubled (see John 14:27). This reveals that when our life feels surrounded by chaos and storms it's the work of the enemy. We need to exert our faith on the fact that living in peace is a God-given promise. That doesn't mean we never face challenges, but it does mean our lives should not be governed by chaos. If you are facing an attack on your peace today, rise up and speak to it. Command every storm to cease and for the chaotic circumstances to settle!

ANOTHER LEVEL
OF GROWTH

DECLARATION

TODAY we declare that you grow and graduate to another level in the spirit. We say that you come into a new degree of spiritual maturity, ability, and understanding. We command every hindering spirit that would come to stunt your growth to be bound in Jesus' Name. We prophesy that you rise from all previous distractions and interruptions and that all areas of spiritual immaturity are replaced by wisdom and readiness. We decree another level of promotion come upon you to elevate you to new places of influence and leadership. We call for every platform that God has designed you to stand upon to manifest in the right timing and nothing shall interfere with it. We say another level of growth develops and comes into full fruition!

SCRIPTURE

Till we all come in the unity of the faith, and of the knowledge of the Son of God, unto a perfect man, unto the measure of the stature of the fulness of Christ: that we henceforth be no more children, tossed to and fro, and carried about with every wind of doctrine, by the sleight of men, and cunning craftiness, whereby they lie in wait to deceive (Ephesians 4:13-14).

WORD OF ENCOURAGEMENT

Believers who do not tend to grow spiritually are those who don't acknowledge they need to grow. While no one would ever come out and bluntly say, "I have arrived," people often unintentionally overlook their own need for personal growth and therefore the result is the same. Personal growth starts by first having a teachable spirit. Then it requires a willingness to acknowledge we can only be trusted with new levels of influence because we humbly recognize the need for constant spiritual development. People who have influence are people who purposefully pursue personal growth. They continually make adjustments. God wants you to grow to another level today so that you can be the most effective person you can be and touch someone's life in a whole new way!

MOUNTAINS REMOVED!

DECLARATION

TODAY we speak to obstacles, mountains, and hindrances and command them to be removed in Jesus' Name. We declare that nothing can stand in the way of answers to prayer, miracles, and breakthroughs. We prophesy to the destroying mountains and say, "The Lord is against you!" We command the high places and strongholds of the enemy to come down from around all that concerns you. We say they shall be entirely moved out of your way, never to be resurrected again. We say every mountain that stands against you shall be brought low and become a plain, and you will not continue to circle the same old mountains and obstacles again. Mountains shall melt like wax at the presence of the Lord that is upon you. We declare you are going over and not going under, for the mountains have been removed!

SCRIPTURE

Who art thou, O great mountain? before Zerubbabel thou shalt become a plain: and he shall bring forth the headstone thereof with shoutings, crying, Grace, grace unto it (Zechariah 4:7).

WORD OF ENCOURAGEMENT

Mountains in Scripture are often metaphorically used to speak of the obstacles we face in life. Jesus taught us to speak to mountains, or the obstacles of life, as an act of faith that we know God is going to make a way for us to overcome (see Mark 11:23). We see this further where Scripture says that mountains melt like wax at the Lord's presence (see Ps. 97:5, Mic. 1:4). In other words, His power causes obstacles to fall. We also see in Jeremiah 51:25, in reference to Babylon's judgement, that God declares He is against the destroying mountain. The point is that God is working alongside your life to remove the obstacles against you, and this happens by our speaking to them. According to the verse above we can look at these mountains and declare grace to them! Our job is to speak to the mountain, and God will see that it moves out of your way!

FINANCIAL
PROVISION COMES NOW!

DECLARATION

WE decree you begin receiving divine and unexpected financial provision to meet every need. We say that debts and deficits are removed and bills are paid on time, every time. We speak that there is financial peace in your life and what has been lacking begins to be filled and supplied. We declare that increase begins to surround your life long term and we declare a settling of all financial problems and issues. We say you receive gainful employment and stable income for your work. In Jesus' Name we bind the enemy's power to create excess breakdowns and repairs causing expenses that rob your resources. We declare financial provision comes now!

SCRIPTURE

But my God shall supply all your need according to his riches in glory by Christ Jesus (Philippians 4:19).

WORD OF ENCOURAGEMENT

I once heard a man say, "There are few things that can create pressure like financial pressure." Of course, while there *are* many other things that truly can create pressure, financial pressure probably makes the top of the list. It's common and everybody, rich or poor, has had financial concerns. Money is by no means the most important thing, but it does affect us daily. God's desire is that you live in financial peace. Of course there are many things we can do to help our financial situation, such as have a gainful career or job that supplies stable income. We should also learn to budget and control spending. Yet there is still that which we can't control. We can't always control our income level or prepare for large, unexpected medical or repair bills. For many people, the best planning efforts can't overcome those things. This is where we must trust God and rely on Him for supernatural supply and also command the enemy to remove his hand of interference. We can ask the Lord to supply His unexpected blessings so even in times of financial need we will experience His supernatural supply. Declare today that financial supply comes now!

ANGELS DESCENDING
AND SURROUNDING

DECLARATION

TODAY we call upon the Lord God of Hosts to commission the reinforcements of His mighty angels to surround your life, your home, family, property, and business. We thank God, according to His promise, that angels have been commissioned to bear you up in their hands so that you will not experience injury, accident, tragedy, or calamity. We call for the angels to protect against all attack, violence, burglary, break-in, mischief, and mayhem. As we speak God's Word, we call for angels to descend and work as ministering servants for us who are heirs of salvation. May angels surround each of your loved ones that they may be safe from all harm and injury. Today we declare in full assurance that angels are standing watch as you sleep and cover you from before and behind. We declare the angels of the Lord are working for you and are on your side!

SCRIPTURE

For he shall give his angels charge over thee, to keep thee in all thy ways. They shall bear thee up in their hands, lest thou dash thy foot against a stone (Psalm 91:11-12).

WORD OF ENCOURAGEMENT

The Bible says in Hebrews 1:14 that angels are sent as ministering servants specifically for God's people. They are here as helpers to keep us safe, but not only that, they help empower us to do what God has called us to do without living in fear of tragedy and harm. We live in a dangerous time in history (see 2 Tim. 3:1), and we need God's angels more than ever! Be assured today that if you stay aware of their activity you will know that they are working on Yahweh's behalf and their purpose will always benefit you. We can ask God to commission angels to stand guard over all that concerns us. Many a praying mother has asked God to send angels to watch over her children. Based on the choices of her kids, you could only assume it was her prayers for God to send angels that kept them safe! Know today, angels are on assignment for you!

YOUR FRUITFUL
SEASON BEGINS NOW

DECLARATION

TODAY we decree that everything that has been locked up and shut up by the enemy is loosed! We declare your days of wilderness and desert living are over! We say you are coming out of every demonic prison constructed unjustly and illegally by the enemy. Every mental block, mind-binding spirit, and every spiritual and physical restriction is broken in the Name of Jesus! We call you loosed from every oppression and we say you are spiritually, emotionally, and physically free! We declare you are loosed to live and breathe and operate in all the fullness and plan of God on every level designed for you. You are like a planted tree that bears fruit against the current of a flowing river. We say *your season of fruitfulness begins now!*

SCRIPTURE

And he shall be like a tree planted by the rivers of water, that bringeth forth his fruit in his season; his leaf also shall not wither; and whatsoever he doeth shall prosper (Psalm 1:3).

WORD OF ENCOURAGEMENT

Fruitfulness is essentially the Bible's description for success. It speaks of productivity and advancement. It's the opposite of decline. If there is anything the enemy wants to get at, it's your sense of accomplishment, whether that is in your personal life, business, or more importantly your Kingdom work and relationship with the Lord. He wants to steal your harvest and will use many means to do so. We need to resist that and know if we live in righteousness and closeness to God, the Bible promises that we shall stand like a tree in a rushing river. Despite the resistance we will keep bearing fruit. Declare today that your barren season is over and that you are entering a whole new era of fruitfulness. Put aside anything that created a hindrance in the past. Rise up today and decree that you *are* going to succeed and bear fruit *now!*

OVERWHELMING LOVE OF THE FATHER

DECLARATION

TODAY we decree that, as a child of God, you experience the overwhelming love of the Father. May you sense His care that covers each of your needs and that you are safe under the shadow of His wings. We bind all feelings of insecurity, abandonment, and rejection in Jesus' Name. May you receive from God a genuine revelation of fatherly love. We pray that the sure arm of God's strength and stability would keep you in complete confidence that He will never leave or forsake you. May your faith be strengthened knowing that He is listening when you call and is quick to answer you when you cry, "Abba, Father!" Yes, you are a child of God and *all* shall be well with you!

SCRIPTURE

*For ye have not received the spirit of bondage again to fear;
but ye have received the Spirit of adoption, whereby we cry,
Abba, Father. The Spirit itself beareth witness with our
spirit, that we are the children of God* (Romans 8:15-16).

WORD OF ENCOURAGEMENT

Children have the natural sense of knowing the care of their
parents. When they have a need, they don't go call for a neighbor. They call for mom and dad! When children grow up in
a safe, loving home they know where to run. Small children
believe Daddy can do anything! While we have the instinct
as natural parents to do anything we can to help our children,
we are also limited human beings. God, however, is not limited and is a limitless, loving Father who wants us to sense His
unfailing love, much the way a young toddler might sense that
from his daddy. When you make the effort to build your
relationship with God as your heavenly Father, it solid-
ifies your faith. This is because you know God loves
you. You also know He will be there for you in your
times of need. Ask Him today to help you sense and
receive a greater revelation of His unfailing love and
the assurance of His care for you as His child!

RELATIONSHIPS
HEALED AND RESTORED

DECLARATION

WE decree that every strained relationship that is not meant to be in your life begins to experience divine healing and restoration. We take authority over the demonic powers of strife, division, anger, and misunderstanding in the Name of Jesus. We declare a disruption and severance from all outside interference and influence that is not from God. May hearts and minds begin to see things from a clearer heavenly perspective. We speak that each person's eyes shall be opened to reason and shall strive for peace. We say that the truth of the Holy Spirit begins to reign upon and change everything that is out of order. We pray that each person involved will turn to God and not rely on the arm of flesh. We decree unity, oneness of mind, love, understanding, forgiveness, grace, and peace. We say that your relationships are healed and restored in Jesus' Name!

SCRIPTURE

Make every effort to keep yourselves united in the Spirit, binding yourselves together with peace (Ephesians 4:3 NLT).

WORD OF ENCOURAGEMENT

Working through relationships is one of life's greatest challenges. Of course, we are not even talking about relationships not meant to be in our lives here. We are talking about those that are, and it can sometimes be a challenge to navigate them. The Bible speaks about striving to find the bond of peace between ourselves and others because we all see things through different lenses. Therefore, it can be hard at times to communicate how we view things. We can try and discuss our differences, and while this has its place, in the end not all things always get solved. This is why we need the Spirit of God to come and bring divine clarity. We need God to help us find that place of peace so that hurt feelings don't eventually become the dominating factor in the relationship. Declare peace over any strained relationships today and allow God to bring His peace so these important relationships can be healed and restored!

VISIONS AND DREAMS FROM GOD

DECLARATION

WE decree that you are positioned to receive divine dreams and visions of God as He desires to bring them upon you. We say that any blockage, hindrance, and demonic interference cannot disrupt your receptivity to heaven's impartation. We call today for the last-days manifestation of dreams and visions to rest upon your life so that you begin to hear from the Spirit in a supernatural way. We declare you have the precise ability to separate natural dreams from spiritual ones. We say that you possess the ability to see and hear accurately into the spirit realm in alignment with the Holy Spirit. May you have dreams of inspiration that give you new ideas, concepts, and thoughts. We call for clear vision and divine imaginations to work within you that shall enable you to accomplish great things. We ask God to allow you to dream dreams and see visions that are given by heaven for this season in Jesus' Name!

SCRIPTURE

And it shall come to pass in the last days, saith God, I will pour out of my Spirit upon all flesh: and your sons and your daughters shall prophesy, and your young men shall see visions, and your old men shall dream dreams: and on my servants and on my handmaidens I will pour out in those days of my Spirit; and they shall prophesy (Acts 2:17-18).

WORD OF ENCOURAGEMENT

One of the key elements of the last days that Peter spoke about on Pentecost in Acts 2 was that God's people would experience the supernatural. Specifically he said that we would experience visions and dreams. Now, while we can't manifest these in our own power, because they are decided and distributed by God, we can ask that this last-days manifestation would have a place in our life. Again, it's as God wills it, but it wouldn't be in Scripture if it wasn't something He didn't want His people to experience. Ask the Lord today to allow you to experience last-days dreams and visions from heaven as He desires!

RESTFUL SLEEP

DECLARATION

WE decree that you begin to experience restful sleep like never before. In Jesus' Name, we break the power of restlessness, sleeplessness, insomnia, tensions, and physical distress that would rob you of a good night's rest. We cast out every nightmare and night terror and we say it cannot operate ever again around you or your home! We speak peace to your mind and body during the night hours. We say that every muscle, bone, cell, organ, and hormone must align itself correctly so you are able to rest. We speak peace to the environment around you and say that you operate in God's promise that He gives His beloved sleep. We speak sweet sleep upon you and may your nights be restful, comfortable, relaxing, and calm. We say that your nights of sleep shall be the best and most rejuvenating yet! Amen!

SCRIPTURE

It is vain for you to rise up early, to sit up late, to eat the bread of sorrows: for so he giveth his beloved sleep (Psalm 127:2).

WORD OF ENCOURAGEMENT

Of all the things one could pray and decree, declaring that you receive a good night of sleep is a priority. There is something about a good night's sleep that seems to make most things better in the morning, and some problems just seem to melt away. It's not that a night of sleep changes a single shred of our circumstances. What sleeping does is change us! When we are rested and rejuvenated everything about us spirit, soul, and body is better able to cope with whatever life hands us. It changes our perspective and gives us the energy to move forward. We certainly know that there are natural things we can do to enhance a good night's sleep, but we often overlook that being unable to sleep can also be spiritual. We need to stand up to the enemy and command all evil forces that would disrupt our ability to rest to leave in Jesus' Name. As you settle in to bed each night, begin declaring over your sleep that it shall be sweet!

OPEN DOORS
AND DIVINE APPOINTMENTS

DECLARATION

WE decree open doors of opportunity, utterance, and divine appointments from heaven come your way. May you be positioned to walk into the right places and situations that set you up for success and influence. We declare that closed doors of rejection shall not be your experience and the only doors that close are those God has closed. We say the enemy has no ability to create blockage and barriers to the places you are destined by God to enter. We declare you receive heavenly appointed phone calls, letters, contacts, contracts, meetings, assignments, platforms, and engagements. We decree that you are given divine opportunities to speak the Word of God and further the Gospel. We call for doors of influence that you didn't even expect and we declare today that a new day of open doors rests upon you!

SCRIPTURE

For a great door and effectual is opened unto me, and there are many adversaries (1 Corinthians 16:9).

WORD OF ENCOURAGEMENT

When the Bible speaks about open doors, it's directly in the context of the spreading of the Gospel and God's purposes going forth (also see Isa. 22:22; 45:11, 2 Cor. 2:12; Rev. 3:7-8). When we ask God to open doors of opportunity or success, it's specifically so we can reach someone for the Lord. Everything we do in our lives should ultimately be with the motivation to further the Kingdom of God. Expanding the Kingdom should be the key reason we want to be successful in everything we do. It shouldn't be something we just keep to ourselves. When we ask God to open doors, we do so with the intent that every open door will provide the opportunity to minister to colleagues, neighbors, loved ones, and friends. Let one of your key declarations each day be that you will walk through open doors!

ENCOUNTERS WITH HIS GLORY

DECLARATION

TODAY we declare that you begin to encounter a new level of God's weight and glory. May you experience the power of His might and majesty on a level that causes you to fall on your knees in humble worship. We say that you supernaturally see His beauty, perfection, depth, and strength. We decree you have a divine revelation of how limitless He is. We declare that you will intimately know the God who created all things, for by Him all things exist and are being upheld by the word of His power. May His goodness pass before you that you will know with certainty that His presence is going with you wherever you go. We prophesy that you will sense His majestic strength in your home, workplace, and community and live and function as a carrier of His great glory. We say that the glory of the Lord will shine all about you and emanate from within you. We prophesy this day that you shall enter into new realms and encounters with His glory, in Jesus' Name!

SCRIPTURE

And the glory which thou gavest me I have given them (John 17:22).

WORD OF ENCOURAGEMENT

Believers commonly talk about the desire to experience the glory of God. It's something everyone who knows God has probably sought. Like Moses in Exodus 33:18, we ask and seek God that we might experience His glory. This craving is an important factor in developing intimacy with an all-powerful God. Yet there is another factor we must include, which is something Jesus prayed. While in the Garden of Gethsemane, Jesus declared that He was giving us the same glory that was upon Him. It sounds extreme, but He was saying that being carriers of God's glory is a promised gift. Through the Holy Spirit within we can *expect* to experience His glory. It's already with us wherever we go! So when we ask to encounter His glory, we are asking for something already promised and therefore we should expect mighty encounters with His glory to manifest!

SATISFIED WITH
LONG, ABUNDANT LIFE

DECLARATION

WE decree that you shall live a long life and shall live to a full age. We declare nothing shall be able to cut your life short. We break the power of early and premature death over you and your loved ones in the Name of Jesus. We say no evil shall be able to end your life before your fullness of days is fulfilled. We prophesy that you live long and strong with days full of strength and vitality. We prophesy that your quality of life is enhanced and that you are filled with physical vigor and stamina. We speak to your whole person—spirit, soul, and body—and say that you are purpose-driven, active, and functioning to your fullest potential. May the God of life move through your entire being so that you shall experience the divine and supernatural life that comes from the Lord. We declare you shall experience as many sunrises and sunsets as your heart desires. We say this day that you shall be satisfied with a long and abundant life!

SCRIPTURE

With long life will I satisfy him, and shew him my salvation (Psalm 91:16).

WORD OF ENCOURAGEMENT

Premature death is a curse. While we can't understand all the factors surrounding why some people "die before their time" or have their life shortened, we can know that God's intent is for His people to experience long, abundant lives. He is the giver of life. Not only does He want us to live long lives, but He wants us to experience quality of life. That is why Psalm 91:16 says we will be *satisfied* with long life. This means we are satisfied with the length of our lives, but also that we are satisfied with the kind of days we experienced. Notice the verse also says God will show us His salvation. The word salvation here is the Hebrew word *yshuw'ah,* or Yeshua, which is the Name *Jesus.* It means delivered, aided, health, saved, and victory. His Name is victory! What does that victory include? Long life and victory over premature death! Declare today that a long, abundant life shall be yours in Jesus' Name!

NEW REALMS OF PRAYER

DECLARATION

WE decree that your prayer life elevates to another level and that you begin to navigate new realms with God. We prophesy that rivers of living water begin to flood from your innermost being. May you enter into the deeper places of communion and fellowship with the Father, Son, and Holy Spirit. We prophesy a new confidence of faith in the things you pray that assures you they shall be answered. We speak a new unlocking in your prayer language that brings about new heavenly dialects as you speak and sing with the tongues of men and of angels. May you pray in unison and cohesion with the Spirit of God, and we decree a new outflow begins to come forth. We break the power of the enemy from trying to disrupt your prayer time and bring unnecessary distractions. We say that your time of prayer shall be sweet, fulfilling, and productive and that you are entering a new level in prayer!

SCRIPTURE

He that believeth on me, as the scripture hath said, out of his belly shall flow rivers of living water (John 7:38).

WORD OF ENCOURAGEMENT

We all know the power of prayer. Without consistent prayer we will experience a gap not only in our intimacy with Him, but also in the force of spiritual power. That is why the enemy works so hard to keep us too busy to find the time for extended prayer that takes us deeper. Our greatest desire is that our prayer life should not stay at status quo, but rather progress and move into new heights. We need to press for a greater prayer experience so the power of the Spirit can flood from within us! Genesis 2:10-14 speaks of four rivers that extended from Eden. With some study we can see how these rivers prophetically point to our prayer experience and how it should be multi-faceted. In these rivers we can see things pertaining to the prayer experience such as quiet streams, fellowship, lengths of time, warfare, and worship—a diverse prayer experience. Make a point to press in to new realms and experiences in your prayer life today!

SET APART AS
A HOLY VESSEL

DECLARATION

TODAY we decree that you are set apart as a holy vessel for the work and purposes of God. We prophesy that you live as a chosen generation, royal priesthood, and holy nation called to manifest His praises. We say you are purged from all contaminants and you are sanctified and separated for the Master's use. We speak that you shall function in the purpose and position God has ordained for you and shall not be sidetracked or inhibited in Jesus' Name. We bind every generational curse from infiltrating your destiny and you shall be found worthy for your divine occupation. We declare you are a vessel that is being beautifully prepared for every Kingdom task and that you have insight into the hope of your heavenly calling and inheritance. We decree you are a holy servant and a refined vessel fully prepared for the work of the Lord!

SCRIPTURE

But in a great house there are not only vessels of gold and of silver, but also of wood and of earth; and some to honour, and some to dishonour. If a man therefore purge himself from these, he shall be a vessel unto honour, sanctified, and meet for the master's use, and prepared unto every good work (2 Timothy 2:20-21).

WORD OF ENCOURAGEMENT

As believers, we carry the responsibility to become refined vessels that are found worthy to represent the Kingdom of God. Many people want to be used by God, but fewer want to put in the effort to allow God to refine them for that purpose. We cannot serve and work for the Lord on our own terms. Where necessary, we need to let Him adjust things like our methods, character, manners, and more. Many people have powerful ministry gifts, but if they lack the etiquette to treat people correctly, their gift becomes stunted. It can't reach its fullest potential until other areas that complement that gift are improved. As you allow God to use you in whatever facet He desires, also allow Him to make adjustments so you can be everything He wants you to become!

DIVINE HEALTH
RESTS UPON YOU

DECLARATION

WE decree that you experience divine health, healing, and wholeness. We take authority over the curse of sickness, disease, viruses, pain, and suffering in Jesus' Name. We command every adverse physical and chronic condition to leave your body and all spirits of infirmity must depart from you. We speak upon you the divine healing promise that Jesus took your sickness and carried your diseases. We say that all meddling ailments, syndromes, disorders, irritations, aches, and discomforts must cease and desist. We speak to your body now and command it to align itself and function the way it was created. We decree you are alleviated from everything that would make you susceptible to disease. We speak and say that your immune system is miraculously strengthened and your health springs forth speedily. We declare it manifests *now* in Jesus' Name!

SCRIPTURE

When the even was come, they brought unto him many that were possessed with devils: and he cast out the spirits with his word, and healed all that were sick: that it might be fulfilled which was spoken by Esaias the prophet, saying, Himself took our infirmities, and bare our sicknesses (Matthew 8:16-17).

WORD OF ENCOURAGEMENT

If there is any promise in the Bible that we need to fight to receive, it's the promise to walk in divine health. Our current world is saturated in various illnesses. It's hard not to run into someone who isn't dealing with some physical condition. Sickness is a curse that robs people of their quality of life; it steals time, money, and more. The Bible is very clear that Jesus came to carry our sicknesses and diseases. However, if we are not careful, we can easily miss out on this promise by not resisting the attack of sickness. We have to be careful not to just tolerate certain conditions either because we have had them a long time or because it just seems like such things are part of life. Jesus paid for us to live in divine health, so it's important that we boldly decree it in His Name!

A FRESH CONFIDENCE

DECLARATION

WE decree right now that you receive a new measure of confidence and courage. We speak that that you live and operate in certainty and assurance about who God has made you. May there be a new morale that comes over your heart and mind. In the Name of Jesus, we break the powers of rejection, shyness, and insecurity from having a voice in your thoughts. May you see yourself in a new light as one who is poised, able, and capable. We say you will not have any hesitation to stand before any person or audience that you are positioned to address. We prophesy that you walk into every circumstance and situation with assurance knowing that you are secure because the Greater One lives within you! We decree no fear and that you are confident in Him!

SCRIPTURE

For the Lord shall be thy confidence, and shall keep thy foot from being taken (Proverbs 3:26).

WORD OF ENCOURAGEMENT

While most wouldn't want admit it, everyone deals with some measure of internal rejection and insecurity. Now this isn't speaking of such a level of insecurity that makes a person completely dysfunctional, but rather certain areas in our minds that make us apprehensive or maybe even fearful. These are the things that often give that sense of feeling unqualified or incapable for some task or situation. Many times, such feelings keep us from taking on certain opportunities. If we are going to rise up and be successful. we need to address the issue of insecurity. One of the best ways to address a lack of confidence is to face it head-on. We need to look at those insecurities in the eye and speak to them! We need to tell ourselves that with God's help we are well qualified. We also need to declare that we won't fail! Last, we must remind ourselves that our confidence comes from the Lord, and if we ask, He will impart a divine confidence into our being that makes all manner of insecurity melt away.

MANIFESTING SIGNS AND WONDERS!

DECLARATION

WE declare that you are one who carries the miraculous upon you and that you operate in the supernatural manifestations of God for this generation. We say that heavenly signs confirm the word that flows from your mouth. We decree that every hindrance and blockage that would prevent the supernatural breaks now in Jesus Name. We take authority over every man-made ideology and empty religious tradition that would keep the mighty works of God from being displayed. We say that you come to know the supernatural attributes of God that enable you to speak with new tongues, cast out demons, and lay hands upon the sick. May you operate in the miraculous power of the Spirit without restraint whenever the need arises. We say signs, wonders, and miracles follow you in Jesus' Name!

SCRIPTURE

Behold, I and the children whom the Lord hath given me are for signs and for wonders (Isaiah 8:18).

WORD OF ENCOURAGEMENT

When Jesus was raised from the dead and ready to return to heaven, He told His disciples that they would carry miraculous faculties upon them as they go out to share the Gospel (see Mark 16:15-18). He told them they would speak in heavenly languages, cast out demons, and lay hands on the infirm so they could be healed. Then after Jesus was received into heaven and the Holy Spirit came upon them at Pentecost, they were endued with the ability to operate in miracles. Mark 16:20 says they went out preaching, and signs and wonders followed them. It's always been the desire of God to manifest the miraculous upon and through His people. We aren't meant to be a powerless church. There is a generation to reach, and they need to see His tangible power! We have been born for signs and for wonders!

DIVINE ENDURANCE

DECLARATION

TODAY we prophesy that a divine ability to endure and overcome rests upon you. We say that you carry the inner fortitude to press forward. We declare you rise up in faith over every trial and test. In Jesus' Name, we declare that you will never give in to the desire to quit or give up! We speak that you are well equipped to endure every difficult situation without falling into frustration. We say the ability to fight the good fight of faith resides strong within you. We break every lie of the enemy that would make you believe that your challenge is so unusual that no one can understand and help. We prophesy that laborers and Kingdom warriors shall be commissioned to help you and encourage you. We say weakness is turned into strength and exhaustion into zeal. We boldly say that you shall endure all hard situations and come out in total victory!

SCRIPTURE

Thou therefore endure hardness, as a good soldier of Jesus Christ (2 Timothy 2:3).

WORD OF ENCOURAGEMENT

One of the oldest tactics of the devil is getting us to feel like quitting. His goal is to make you think you can't go another step. If we allow that, we will begin saying and believing all the wrong things. We will believe there is no end in sight to the thing we are fighting, so why try? If you've ever felt like giving up, then that should serve as a sign that you shouldn't. Never believe there isn't a light at the end of the tunnel. Remind yourself of all the feats of faith others have endured. In fact, Hebrews 11 is a compilation of just that. The minute we think we have endured the worst, there is always someone out there who has gone through just the same or worse. Reminding ourselves of this isn't meant to minimize our battle, it reminds us that we *can* keep going and know there are others out there who have made it through. We can keep going because we know God will give the divine ability to endure so we can come out in victory.

A SONG IN YOUR HEART

DECLARATION

WE decree that your heart is filled with song. May you well up with rejoicing, celebration, joy, and singing. May you become overjoyed for the marvelous things the Lord has done. We break the power of all sadness and gloominess that would steal the song in your heart. We say that every spirit of defeat is bound and not allowed to fill your mind in Jesus' Name. May the song in your heart overtake all negative emotions and give you a renewed sense of confident victory. We prophesy that you receive new songs inspired by the Holy Spirit that declare the wonderful works of God in your life. We declare you receive new revelation through song. We decree songs, new songs, hymns, spiritual songs, and melodies come forth from within you, all to the glory and praise of the Lord. May the song of the Lord well up within you today!

SCRIPTURE

Oh, sing to the Lord a new song, for He has done marvelous deeds! His right hand and His holy arm have accomplished deliverance (Psalm 98:1 MEV).

WORD OF ENCOURAGEMENT

There is something about singing that pushes the dark clouds away. Song and music have a unique ability to make a person feel better about their circumstances or about life in general. We see with the psalmist David how he would often depict the struggles of his life in the Book of Psalms. We have to, however, remind ourselves that those were songs from his heart. Perhaps when he wrote about those struggles and prayers to God it would help him feel a sense of assurance when he sang those words as opposed to just saying them. The point is that song can dispel feelings of defeat. Music can add joy to a room and change the atmosphere. Song can carry with it a delivering power. Declare that your heart will be full of song, so when you're facing a challenge your tendency will be to hum a tune or sing to the Lord. Song is a weapon of victory, so never allow the enemy to steal the song in your heart!

SAFE TRAVEL
AND TRANSIT

DECLARATION

WE decree that you are safe in all manner of travel, transport, and transit. May every vehicle or any method you use to commute be safe and delivered from breakdown or accident. We prophesy that when you walk your foot shall not stumble or fall. You are safe when you come in and when you go out. We call for the angelic hosts to come and protect you from all harm. In Jesus' Name, we declare that all spirits of harassment, hindrance, tragedy, or calamity are forbidden to operate against you when you travel or commute. We say the angels will hold every vehicle or method of transport in their hands. We declare that you will always reach your intended destinations safely and in peace. We say your paths and routes are always divinely guided by the hand of the Lord. We decree that all travel is safe and secure in Jesus' Name!

SCRIPTURE

Blessed shalt thou be when thou comest in, and blessed shalt thou be when thou goest out (Deuteronomy 28:6).

WORD OF ENCOURAGEMENT

There is probably not one person who doesn't think about travel safety. Even non-believers think about their safety and will look at natural ways to ensure they reach every destination safely. We all do important things like wear seatbelts, obey traffic laws, and so forth, but those of us who know God can also rely on the power of prayer to keep us safe as we come and go. Deuteronomy 28:6 reminds us of God's promise to provide travel safety. We can decree and ask the Lord to provide safety from the moment we leave our front door each day and expect that to rest upon us until we return and thereafter. Expecting heavenly protection as we go about life whether by car or some other method of travel is a biblical promise that we should regularly declare and think upon. Wake up each day expecting to reach every destination in safety and peace, not only for yourself but also for your loved ones!

A SWORD IN YOUR MOUTH!

DECLARATION

WE decree the sword of the Lord is in your mouth. May the things you speak be filled with divine truth and heavenly revelation. We prophesy that your words carry power to bless, heal, deliver, and exhort. May you be anointed to speak with taste and grace, class and poise. We declare you receive confidence when you open your mouth that you always know what to say and how to share it. We pray that the Lord places a watch over your lips to prevent you from speaking anything contrary to what is right and godly. We decree that your words shall be a polished weapon against the forces of darkness. We prophesy that your words are filled with heavenly authority and capture the attention of your hearers. May you know when to speak and when to refrain from speaking, and we say an anointing comes upon your speech enabling you to speak a right word in due season as the sword of heaven comes from your mouth!

SCRIPTURE

And he hath made my mouth like a sharp sword; in the shadow of his hand hath he hid me, and made me a polished shaft; in his quiver hath he hid me (Isaiah 49:2).

WORD OF ENCOURAGEMENT

One of our most key instruments as representatives of the Gospel is found in our words. It was said of Jesus that His words carried power and authority (see Luke 4:32). There was obviously something unique anytime Jesus opened His mouth to speak. His words had the power to cast out demons, heal the sick, and calm the storms. We also know that our words carry power (see Prov. 18:21). However, even with power in our words we can't be fully effective unless we know how to use our words correctly. We need to allow the Lord to polish the things that come from our mouth so we can speak for the Lord with not only power, but tastefully and accurately. Decree today that your words are divinely anointed and that the sword of the Lord is in your mouth!

TRUSTED
FRIENDSHIPS

DECLARATION

WE declare that you begin to experience godly and trusted friendships. We say that every acquaintance or relationship in your life that is not from God is interrupted and disrupted in the Name of Jesus. We break the enemy's power from planting any person in your life who has a wrong agenda or toxic behaviors. In Jesus' Name we break the powers of witchcraft from inserting the wrong people in your life. We break the powers of abandonment, guilt, betrayal, and alienation from your soul. We prophesy that you possess within you the ability to trust others. We decree that you will always enjoy friendships with godly people who are trustworthy and reliable. May the Lord send the right people into your life so that you are surrounded by wholesome relationships that edify. We decree you shall not live in loneliness and shall not ever feel that you don't have supportive friends around you in your times of need. We say that your life is filled with trusted friendships!

SCRIPTURE

Iron sharpens iron, so a man sharpens the countenance of his friend (Proverbs 27:17 MEV).

WORD OF ENCOURAGEMENT

The ability to find and build solid friendships in one's life is something every person desires. No one wants to be surrounded by people they can't trust. Betrayal has been a key element in why many people lack trust in others and often shy away from genuine and healthy relationships. God wants you to believe that He will send the right people into your life who will edify you, have your back, and more importantly pray for you. They will be those who won't tear you down and take away from you, but rather sharpen you and make you a better person. If you're carrying any lack of trust within because someone didn't treat you correctly, then give it over to the Lord and begin to decree and have faith that God will begin bringing the right people along your path!

STRONG AND RESILIENT

DECLARATION

WE declare that you receive supernatural strength to endure the pressures of this life. We prophesy you are strong, resilient, and firm. We decree you are able to withstand in the evil day without buckling. We say that you rise up in the power of God's might so that you are able to wage war successfully against principalities, powers, rulers of darkness, and spiritual wickedness in heavenly places. We command all intense stress, pressure, mayhem, and chaos to be alleviated in the Name of Jesus! We decree you will not faint or grow weary and that anxiety has no hold over you. You shall not look around you in terror or fear. We prophesy that the Spirit of the Lord will harden you to difficulty and you shall see the Lord's help upon and around you. We declare today that you bounce back from every challenge and that you stand up strong!

SCRIPTURE

Fear not [there is nothing to fear], for I am with you; do not look around you in terror and be dismayed, for I am your God. I will strengthen and harden you to difficulties, yes, I will help you; yes, I will hold you up and retain you with My [victorious] right hand of rightness and justice (Isaiah 41:10 AMPC).

WORD OF ENCOURAGEMENT

One of the greatest attributes a person can possess is resilience. To be able to walk through something challenging or even painful and be able to bounce back and turn that test into a testimony is a tremendous testament to your character. However, we need the Spirit of God to impart His supernatural resiliency within. Without Him we can do nothing, and we need Him to impart His strength. Through His power He can harden us to the difficulty so that we aren't scarred by the storm. We may have faced the storm, but it carries no lasting impact on our future. However, we still need to decide internally that we will press in until our challenge becomes a victory and our test becomes a testimony. Don't underestimate yourself or the resilience God has put within you today!

NO FEAR OF MAN

DECLARATION

WE decree that all fear of man is broken from your life. You shall not carry a concern or any manner of anxiety of what others might say or do against you. We declare that all forms of intimidation and any sense of threat in your mind are driven from you. We prophesy that no assailant, antagonist, abuser, invader, or aggressor shall ever be able to touch you or come against you in the Name of Jesus! We speak that you are loosed from the strong arm of any person who has set themselves as an enemy and we declare, "Peace!" We decree over your mind and say that your thoughts are immersed in the help of the Lord that is around you right now preventing any evil. We decree a confidence in the Lord's defense that is working on your behalf enabling you to say, "What can man do to me?" From this day forward all fear of man is broken from your life!

SCRIPTURE

The Lord is with me; I will not be afraid. What can mere mortals do to me? (Psalm 118:6 NIV)

WORD OF ENCOURAGEMENT

This verse in the Book of Psalms is particularly powerful in the fact that it comes across as if the writer is being suddenly hit with an amazing thought or mental epiphany. Reading it, you could almost paraphrase it like this: "Wait a minute! What am I so worked up about? God is here! Mere humans cannot hurt me!" We have to remind ourselves of this fact because when someone begins to act out antagonistically toward us it can be a normal response to become fearful of what the outcome could possibly be. Whether it's a legitimate situation or the fear of something that *could* happen, we need to make a point to break the fear of man from our lives. We need to exercise continual faith in the fact that God is always with us; He is for us and is going to take care of us. Like the psalmist, we need to assert our confidence and say out loud, "What can man do to me?"

INSTRUCTION AND INTELLIGENCE

DECLARATION

TODAY we decree you receive revelation and instruction from the Lord. We declare that it becomes easy for you to receive wisdom, teaching, information, and ideas. We say that every mental block or intellectual gap is broken and your mind is able to comprehend and understand. We prophesy that a brilliancy and intelligence of mind comes upon you. We decree you have the capacity to reason correctly and make good judgments. We say that your memory is blessed and that it functions at its full measure. We pray for supernatural teaching from the Lord to permeate your mind and your heart. May the Great Instructor teach you His ways regarding the important elements and situations surrounding your life that keep you steps ahead of the enemy. We break the power of any distraction that would prevent you from keeping the Lord as the center of your learning processes. We say that you function in the intelligent ability the Lord has given you and that His instruction is upon you!

SCRIPTURE

Teach me thy way, O Lord, and lead me in a plain path, because of mine enemies (Psalm 27:11).

WORD OF ENCOURAGEMENT

One of the great abilities the Lord has given us is the use of our mind. He gave us the capacity to learn and absorb information. It is healthy for us to spend time learning and to exercise our brain through study or observation. However, even the brightest geniuses in the world will be shown as profoundly inadequate without the Lord's instruction guiding the learning process. Without His instruction we become reliant on the fallacies of our own human concepts. Ask the Lord to bring His instruction into your life. As you study, whether that be the Bible or other subject matter, do not forget the important element of calling on the Lord, the Great Instructor, to not only teach you His knowledge, but to also teach you His divine ways in how to apply what you learn.

UNITY WITH THE BODY OF CHRIST

DECLARATION

WE declare that you live in harmony and unity with your fellow believers. We prophesy that a sense of kinship resides in your spirit that enables you to maintain oneness with your brothers and sisters in Christ. May you be able to properly discern the Lord's Body in truth and love. We say the power of misunderstanding, division, miscommunication, and discord are broken and replaced by communication, understanding, and agreement. May you be able to find places of peace and harmony even with those with whom you cannot see eye to eye on certain viewpoints. May you be free from any hurts or feelings of betrayal caused by a brother or sister in the Lord. May the ability to forgive be the element that reigns supreme in your heart, and we say you experience the pleasantness that comes from being united. We decree you are able to effectively function in the local church body and supply a positive contribution to the Kingdom of God. May your unity with the Body of Christ descend like the oil of the Holy Spirit upon your life in Jesus' Name!

SCRIPTURE

Behold, how good and how pleasant it is for brethren to dwell together in unity! (Psalm 133:1)

WORD OF ENCOURAGEMENT

Before Jesus was crucified, one of His prayers was that His brethren would be united (see John 17:11). As believers we are called the *Body* of Christ, which reveals we are to function in harmony. A divided body is unhealthy, and that is why we must strive for unity. Obviously, we will not all agree on everything. We may see certain Scriptures differently, misunderstand another's intentions, or even feel hurt by someone in the church. Even in Scripture we see where the early church dealt with differences. This is why during communion, Paul said we are to discern the Lord's Body (see 1 Cor. 11:27-29). Make a point to strive for oneness and ask the Lord to help you be a unifier in His Body!

DECLARATION FOR ISRAEL

DECLARATION

WE decree over the nation of Israel the word, "Peace!" We speak peace, safety, and security over Israel. May every enemy set against them be disrupted and interrupted from their evil intent. May the Lord cause Israel to retain all the land that is rightfully theirs. We pray that the nations would be at peace with Israel and that they would be free from unfair political maneuvers and agreements. We prophesy a supernatural peace to come upon the citizens so that they live free from dread and fear. We say that the Gospel shall go forth in Israel unhindered and with great success and the word of God shall not return void. We pray the Lord would cause His blessing to be upon you, Israel, and may your friends, neighbors, and even your enemies see the unique and supernatural hand of God upon you. We say Israel and Jerusalem are prosperous, blessed, and safe in Jesus' Name!

SCRIPTURE

Pray for the peace of Jerusalem: they shall prosper that love thee (Psalm 122:6).

WORD OF ENCOURAGEMENT

Even the secular world should recognize that there is something unique about Israel. This tiny little nation in the Middle East is the constant topic in modern-day news. It is the continual target by Arab nations and has a history that draws attention like none other. Additionally, Israel is one of the few nations still in a vehement war over territorial dividing lines. We also know, biblically speaking, Israel is a focus point that many use to gauge end-time events. All of this further reveals that we should pray for Israel and for Jerusalem because what happens there effects the world. As the next events unfold, our prayers for God's people in the land of Israel are so important. We are taught in Scripture to pray for their peace and safety and that all who love them will be blessed of the Lord. Declare peace upon Israel and you will be blessed!

PRODIGALS RETURNING

DECLARATION

WE decree that your prodigal, backslidden, and wayward children and family members return to God. We decree that they receive revelation in the knowledge of God that brings them back into a right relationship with the Lord. We prophesy that their eyes and ears are open to truth. We break the power of every seducing, lying, and deceiving spirit in Jesus' Name. We say that any hard-heartedness, stiff-necked resistance, or rebellious spirit is broken. We command all curses of witchcraft holding them captive to be destroyed by the anointing. We declare that Gospel laborers shall be placed in their path to minister truth and life. We speak that hearts become opened and softened to the Holy Spirit. They shall return to fellowship with the Body of Christ and all relationships that would influence with evil are severed. We break every soul tie to wrong relationships, habits, and places and we declare the prodigals come home now and that a time of celebration begins!

SCRIPTURE

For this my son was dead, and is alive again; he was lost, and is found (Luke 15:24).

WORD OF ENCOURAGEMENT

One of the hardest challenges believers face is when they have a loved one who has drifted away from God. Standing by and seeing them go down a wrong road is painful. The encouraging thing to remember is that God is always pulling for the backslider. Hosea 14:4 says that God loves the backslider. Even though they have made terrible mistakes, the Lord is continually wooing them back to Himself. As a family member standing by, our job is to continue praying. As hard as it can be not to, we can't put excess pressure upon them to make changes. We certainly can admonish when opportunities arise, but we can't force anyone or nag them. We can pray, be an example, and most certainly decree into the atmosphere their supernatural return back into the Kingdom of God!

FREE FROM
THE CURSE

DECLARATION

WE prophesy that the curse has no place or ability to function or raise its head against your life. It cannot function in your home, on your property, or in your family in the Name of Jesus. We break the power of every generational curse, iniquity, or generational sin. We say that you and your bloodline are curse-free and that every curse is replaced with the generational blessing. Every element of family history that was birthed through sin and wickedness shall cease and desist and not continue to the future generations. We prophesy that going forward you shall live in the blessing and experience favor. Your mind is free from the effect of past curses and you shall no longer give time, attention, or concern to the previous curse. We decree you are curse-free!

SCRIPTURE

Christ hath redeemed us from the curse of the law, being made a curse for us: for it is written, Cursed is every one that hangeth on a tree (Galatians 3:13).

WORD OF ENCOURAGEMENT

What we often refer to as generational curses are the negative issues that exist in our family tree or bloodline. They typically enter because of the choices of our parents, grandparents, and in certain cases go back as far as our distant ancestors. Because these curses or issues have often been with us our whole lives and can seem monumental, we often just learn to accept them rather than work to change them. Remember that Jesus bore the curse when He hung on the tree! When you see negative patterns, sin habits, or sicknesses that seem to be repeatedly passed down through your family members, begin to address any curse that may be getting transferred to the next generation. Begin speaking against the curses that have affected your life, family, and bloodline and expect to see them broken today!

A WELL-DESERVED BREAK!

DECLARATION

WE decree you come into a season that is devoid of intense warfare and constant struggle. We prophesy that you experience an obvious and sudden moment of reprieve and alleviation from your battles. May you look about you in this moment and find that every enemy and attack is nowhere to be found. We declare a supernatural rest from your enemies and we speak that you enter into a well-deserved break that comes from the Lord! We speak that a season to build and progress comes upon you. Within you arises a refreshed ability to pause and enjoy life, relax, and unwind. We say that you pause to know God in a fresh new way. May your experience with the Lord become saturated with a sweet, gentle wind from the Spirit. We prophesy a calm serenity to surround you and may you return with renewed fire, zeal, and energy. We say a time to take a break and recharge comes upon you supernaturally right now!

SCRIPTURE

But now the Lord my God hath given me rest on every side, so that there is neither adversary nor evil occurrent (1 Kings 5:4).

WORD OF ENCOURAGEMENT

King David was a man in so much warfare that He couldn't build the temple for the Lord, even though it was in his heart to do so. However, Solomon reigned in a season of peace and was able to build it. The point is when you are in constant warfare, battle after battle, you can't build and progress because you are so busy fighting. Perhaps this is where you are in your life right now. Or, maybe you aren't experiencing spiritual warfare specifically, but you are just exhausted from the stresses of life and need a recharge. Know that God *does* want you to have moments to pull back and be able to pause. God wants you to be able to get renewed and let your uptight muscles relax a little so you can build toward the necessary positive elements for the future. Ask the Lord for a well-deserved and supernaturally given break today!

HIS
PERFECT WILL

DECLARATION

WE decree that the perfect will of God is being established in your life. We prophesy that you will never miss God's plan, direction, and path. We break the power of any fear that would make you anxious about making a mistake. We say of every fork in the road before you, causing you to feel uncertain about the next steps—the choice on where to go is made clear. We say you know God's perfect will concerning your family, job, finances, health, home, and calling. We declare you are sure-footed and assured of your choices and decisions as you follow God's plan. We say that your mind is renewed and you possess the ability to prove the good, acceptable, and perfect will of God. We say that you live and function in His perfect will and nothing shall be able to interfere in Jesus' Name!

SCRIPTURE

And be not conformed to this world: but be ye transformed by the renewing of your mind, that ye may prove what is that good, and acceptable, and perfect, will of God (Romans 12:2).

WORD OF ENCOURAGEMENT

Having the confidence of being in God's perfect will is one of the most fulfilling feelings. It boosts your faith that you are not only doing the right thing, but it gives the inner strength to put a full effort into whatever is before you. On the other hand, being unsure of God's will can be terrifying. It makes you lack confidence to move ahead in your endeavors. A key way to be sure of God's perfect will comes by avoiding conformity to the world. That means not being overly immersed in worldly environments. Things like too many secular friendships and alliances or perhaps too much information from sources devoid of a godly perspective can all make hearing God's will difficult. Filling yourself instead with resources from a godly perspective will help you locate the will of God. Then lastly, always ask the Lord to show you His perfect will for you!

NEVER
FORSAKEN

DECLARATION

WE decree that you will never live with a feeling of being alone or forsaken. We say that whenever you face a challenge, the enemy is not able to speak lies that you are isolated and forgotten. We break the power of any feelings of abandonment, betrayal, desertion, or rejection in Jesus' Name. We prophesy that you will never live as an outcast or lonely and will always know that you are needed and wanted. We speak that you are surrounded by the protection and care from God's loving hand. We say that you have friends and alliances that remind you that you are loved, appreciated, and deeply valued. We say that your mind carries that constant awareness that God will never leave your side and will always be with you wherever you go. We say you are never forsaken and you are always remembered and accepted in the Name of Jesus!

SCRIPTURE

Thou shalt no more be termed Forsaken; neither shall thy land any more be termed Desolate: but thou shalt be called Hephzibah, and thy land Beulah: for the Lord delighteth in thee, and thy land shall be married (Isaiah 62:4).

WORD OF ENCOURAGEMENT

The feeling or sense of being alone is very real and can be most terrifying. Some can feel this more than others depending on their unique circumstances, but truth is everyone has had times of feeling isolated on some level. Even though we know God is there, we can still feel alone. However, the feeling of being alone is not what God wants for us. In fact, He created humankind because He didn't want to be alone; He wanted our fellowship. God made Eve because He didn't want Adam to be alone. Times of feeling alone will affect every person, but it's important not to allow feelings of being alone or loneliness to consume your mind and overtake you. Decree against any method the enemy might be using to make you feel lonely, isolated, or forsaken, and remember today you are deeply loved not only by God but by someone in this world today!

NEW
IDENTITY

DECLARATION

TODAY we decree that you receive and live in a new identity that is saturated in Christ. We speak that the former things that labeled you are removed and have passed away and can no longer define you. We bind the work of all previous characterizations that would tether you to the past and cause you to be seen as something that you are not. We say the former "you" is crucified and a new "you" has arisen! We sever from your memory any past images of yourself that are not in line with the image of Christ. We speak that your new identity is visible to you and all those around you. We say that your new character speaks for itself and shall bring you assurance, adulation, and acceptance. We prophesy that the new person God has made you shall show forth brightly and others shall come to the brightness upon you. We say you are a new person—the old is gone and brand new has come!

SCRIPTURE

Therefore if any man be in Christ, he is a new creature: old things are passed away; behold, all things are become new (2 Corinthians 5:17).

WORD OF ENCOURAGEMENT

When we give our lives over to Jesus, the Bible tells us we became a brand-new creature. This means we are not what we used to be. We are completely different in nature, character, and even our DNA, spiritually speaking, has changed. The joy and sense of this new identity is second to none! However, the enemy will try to put you back and paint you in the former season. He will try to get you immersed in who you used to be, not who you are now. He might try to remind you of your past and also use others to label you in your past. Rise up and receive your new identity in Christ today and don't allow the thoughts and images of who you were to come back to haunt you. Rise up today and declare, "I have a new identity in Jesus' Name!"

BORN TO STAND OUT

DECLARATION

WE decree you shall not live your days blending in but standing out. We say you shall shine and be promoted to represent the Kingdom. May you only experience the seasons of hiding that come from the Lord and not those that come from the enemy, who would try and keep you pushed down and held back. We decree you are being drawn out of obscurity into God's limelight of influence. We say that the unique role that you have been ordained by God to play comes to its fullest measure of effectiveness. We say you have been born for such a time as this and you shall stand out with a unique message and anointing. We say people are drawn to you and that you shall excel and emerge into an exceptional vessel of His glory and that the Name of the Lord shall be glorified in you and through you. You are born to stand out!

SCRIPTURE

Even for this same purpose have I raised thee up, that I might shew my power in thee, and that my name might be declared throughout the earth (Romans 9:17).

WORD OF ENCOURAGEMENT

God has established a place of prominence for every person. While our places of prominence vary from person to person, each has a God-ordained circle of influence. Even if that influence is to a neighbor or co-worker, God wants to make you exceptional in that realm and stand out in that arena. Jesus didn't call us to blend in and live in obscurity. We need to be people who can tastefully and gracefully stand out to others, carry a stand-out message, and walk with God's power upon us in a unique way. The early church was noted for standing out with notable messages and uncommon miracles. We are no different; God wants His people to stand out. Ask God to make you a stand-out individual today, not with an attitude of selfish ambition, but rather so you can represent the Kingdom of God with influence!

TIME FOR
A PRAISE BREAK!

DECLARATION

WE decree that you find continual reasons to pause and give God a shout of praise. We say you see past every element of opposition and find a place of praise. May there be a shout in your mouth, rejoicing in your heart, dancing in your feet, and a clap in your hands. We decree you are quick to fall on your knees in worship. We say you are released into mighty and crazy praise. We declare nothing can steal your praise; no demon or evil spirit can steal your praise. No person or circumstance can rob your praise. We prophesy that you are impacted by sudden and overwhelming praises that well up from within. We speak that you are given to pause from what you are doing and take a moment to praise. We declare you see all the reasons around you that spark your praise. We say that you shall see the glorious greatness of your God in every situation and you will be overcome to pause and take a praise break!

SCRIPTURE

Great is the Lord and most worthy of praise; his greatness no one can fathom (Psalm 145:3 NIV).

WORD OF ENCOURAGEMENT

Even though we know deep down that God is most deserving of our praise, sometimes we can go through the day and forget to actively look for reasons to praise Him. Finding reasons to praise is something we need to make a conscious habit of doing. If we don't, we can easily become so immersed in our circumstances that we allow them to blind us from seeing how great God is in the midst of it. We fail to see all God is doing in the little things. Make an effort to look for opportunities for praise. Not every pause for praise requires a loud outburst, especially if you are in public or at work; it can be a whisper or a joyful prayer. Then there are times when no one is around and you need to express praise with your whole being! The key is to find continual reasons to pause for a praise break and refuse to let anything steal your praise!

LIFE MORE ABUNDANT

DECLARATION

WE decree that you live a life filled with abundance. We say your quality of life improves and excels. May the abundant life of the Lord Jesus surround you. We declare that no evil spirit of lack or depletion can interrupt the abundance and sufficiency God has supplied for you. Every thief that would come to steal, kill, or destroy is bound in the Name of Jesus! We prophesy that insufficiency is turned into plenty. We declare you live with nothing missing and nothing broken. We say you live abundantly spiritually, physically, and emotionally. We say you have financial sufficiency and are bountiful in goods. May the joy and fun of living your life rest wholly upon you. We speak that you are able to do all the wonderful things you desire and are able to do so with strength and stamina. We declare that you have all sufficiency in all things and God's grace for plentiful living abounds toward you!

SCRIPTURE

The thief cometh not, but for to steal, and to kill, and to destroy: I am come that they might have life, and that they might have it more abundantly (John 10:10).

WORD OF ENCOURAGEMENT

Living in abundance is a biblical promise. It isn't just about financial abundance, but rather having a quality of life. Of course there is an element of financial blessing that is part of that, but God wants us to have abundance in all areas. What good is having lots of money if you are emotionally imbalanced or bound by some incurable illness? That wouldn't be an abundant life either. Jesus came and declared a promise of abundance and He made it clear it's the enemy who comes to rob us of that. The enemy comes to take your joy of living by inundating you with difficulties. Declare in faith today that you will always live in God's promises for abundance and that you will always have a good quality of life!

NO MORE
SHAME

DECLARATION

WE decree that the shame and reproach of your youth is driven from you in the Name of Jesus. We say that all manner of shame from a past season is broken off your life. May your years of youthful foolishness and immaturity be forgotten and replaced by a new season of prudence and wisdom. We say you come into your full age of maturity in the spirit. May those around you see the thoughtfulness and sensibility that rests upon you in this new season. We speak that an anointing comes upon you to provide wisdom and admonishment to others in their personal journey of growth. We speak that people, places, and circumstances shall not bring you into the condemnation of a former season of immaturity. May nothing remind you of what used to be and may you only think of where God is bringing you. We prophesy that the shame of your youth is broken and shall never return to you again!

SCRIPTURE

Fear not; for thou shalt not be ashamed: neither be thou confounded; for thou shalt not be put to shame: for thou shalt forget the shame of thy youth, and shalt not remember the reproach of thy widowhood any more (Isaiah 54:4).

WORD OF ENCOURAGEMENT

To think of what you used to be like in your younger years can often trigger thoughts of embarrassment. People often joke about their teen or early adulthood as they relate some of the foolish choices they made at that time. However, even as we advance in years we can all still experience times when we wish we had done some things differently. Maybe it was how we treated someone or handled a situation and we realize we could have done better or used more maturity. Release any shame that has held your mind captive right now and realize you can't change the past, but you can change the future. You can choose to make better decisions going forward. We serve a powerful God who can release us from the shame of our past as if it never happened!

HIS BODY
AND BLOOD

DECLARATION

W E decree you receive a new understanding and revelation of the Body and Blood of Christ. May the understanding of the communion meal be increased within you. We say each time you receive of the Body and Blood of our Lord in His supper that your inner being is saturated with the supernatural power that is provided in this meal. We say it causes healing, and as you receive, we declare all poisons and toxins are driven from your mind and your body. We say you are washed afresh with the cleansing blood of Jesus. May you have a clear ability to receive the supper of the Lord and be able to correctly examine yourself and also discern the Lord's Body according to the Word of God. May the communion meal become real to you and cause you to receive a revelation of the Lord Jesus and His death and resurrection in a life-changing way. We prophesy that all the benefits provided in the meal of the Lord rest upon you, within you, and around you in Jesus' Name.

SCRIPTURE

And when he had given thanks, he brake it, and said, Take, eat: this is my body, which is broken for you: this do in remembrance of me (1 Corinthians 11:24).

WORD OF ENCOURAGEMENT

The communion meal is far more than just a ceremonial practice. It's a directive from the Lord that carries within it supernatural power. Jesus instructed that we are to do it in His remembrance. What is the power of that? Each time we remember His death and resurrection we are recalling what it provided us. We remember that He died and with Him our own sins were buried. We remember that when He rose, we rose with Him into a newness of life, not just in the life to come, but right now. The communion meal represents the supernatural power of the cross, and each time we receive it, we take that supernatural power within us. It's also a time for self-examination and forgiveness of others. There is power in this holy meal and we decree that power goes into you today!

THE LIVING
WORD OF GOD

DECLARATION

WE decree today that the living Word of God dwells in you richly with all wisdom and truth. We say that you are removed from the vain philosophies of the day and that you are clothed with the Word of Truth found in the Scriptures. We say you are drawn to give your full attention to His Word and that you meditate upon it in your heart and mind. We say your ear is inclined to hear God's sayings from the Bible and that you do not let them depart from your eyes and that you keep them in the midst of your heart. May the Word of God that is alive and active be like a sword upon your lips so you will be driven to speak His Word continually. We say the angels of the Lord are activated to the sound of God's Word spoken from your mouth. May the living Word of God wash you, cleanse you, and fill you with faith. We prophesy that the Word of God shall permeate you with power, truth, and life in Jesus' Name!

SCRIPTURE

My son, attend to my words; incline thine ear unto my sayings. Let them not depart from thine eyes; keep them in the midst of thine heart. For they are life unto those that find them, and health to all their flesh. Keep thy heart with all diligence; for out of it are the issues of life (Proverbs 4:20-23).

WORD OF ENCOURAGEMENT

The foundational point of reference to our Christianity is found in the Bible. The written Word of God is what determines truth and boundaries. It builds our level of faith. It admonishes and corrects. Without the Word of God hidden in our hearts, we have no point of reference to determine the way and will of God. As you decree today, declare that the Word of God is rich within you. Doing so will develop in you a hunger for the Scriptures and it will become the resource that will cause you to be a well-balanced, discerning believer. It will give you a thirst to make time in the Bible a priority. The Word of God will saturate you with life, healing, faith, and hope. Become hungry for His living Word every day!

ANTICIPATING HIS COMING

DECLARATION

WE decree that you never lose sight of His glorious second coming! May you continue to anticipate the return of our Lord, for your redemption draws near. May those in this day who mock and ignore the day of the Lord's return have no ability to sway your focus and expectation to see Jesus. We break the power of all dimness of vision, distraction, and lethargy that would remove your eyes from your heavenly reward. May you be in line with the Scriptures that declare, "Come quickly, Lord Jesus!" We say you are found among the faithful saints who anticipate His appearing. We declare you are a vessel prepared with oil in your lamp awaiting the bridegroom. We decree you are one in whom the day of the Lord shall not overtake you as a thief, but that you will be ready and expectant at all times. May a renewed excitement for the Lord's soon return well up from within you and may the joy of His coming refresh you today!

SCRIPTURE

Nevertheless we, according to his promise, look for new heavens and a new earth, wherein dwelleth righteousness (2 Peter 3:13).

WORD OF ENCOURAGEMENT

A few decades ago, you didn't have to look far to hear a sermon that carried the message that Jesus is coming soon. Nowadays these sermons are less common, yet we are closer to His coming than ever. If there is anything that we need more of, it's a greater anticipation of the Lord's return. The Bible tells us that His return should not hit us by surprise (see 1 Thess. 5:4). We are supposed to be in a place of daily expectation regarding His coming. Like the five wise virgins in Matthew 25, we should have oil in our lamps ready to meet the bridegroom. That means we should be constantly preparing our lives to meet Jesus. We have to be careful that we don't let all the busyness and distractions of this life take our eyes off that fact that Jesus' return is imminent. We must always be able to say, "Come quickly, Lord Jesus!"

ASSURED FAITH

DECLARATION

WE decree you receive an assured faith that provides you the proof of the things you are hoping for and praying about. Through the eye of faith, we declare you are able to see the things that you cannot see with your natural eye. We break the power of all unbelief, doubt, fear, and faithlessness in the Name of Jesus. We speak to every opposing circumstance that would try to dissuade your confidence that what you are praying for shall manifest. We say your faith is unshakable and unmovable and becomes your proof of the facts. We prophesy that you know beyond any shadow of doubt that the Lord has heard your prayers, heaven is moving, and miracles are in motion. We say your faith shall be assured and you shall not be anxious for anything, but shall rest in the fact that your requests are being heard in the throne room of grace. We prophesy an assurance of faith to rest and remain upon you today!

SCRIPTURE

Now faith is the assurance (the confirmation, the title deed) of the things [we] hope for, being the proof of things [we] do not see and the conviction of their reality [faith perceiving as real fact what is not revealed to the senses] (Hebrews 11:1 AMPC).

WORD OF ENCOURAGEMENT

The Bible makes it very clear that we are not supposed to live focused only on what we can see with our natural eye. In fact our very Christianity is based on this truth. We love, serve, and believe in the Lord, although we can't physically see Him. It's the same regarding the things we pray about. We may not see the answer yet, but we can be assured of it through the eye of faith. Hebrews 11:1 says faith becomes the proof long before we see the manifestation of the answer in the natural realm. If you have gotten discouraged while waiting for an answer to prayer, work on strengthening your faith. Decree over your faith today that you will not lose hope, but rather that your faith will remain assured!

A SHARP
MEMORY

DECLARATION

WE decree you have a sharp and healthy memory. We declare your mind is able to recall and recount with accuracy and precision. We prophesy that your mind is blessed and that no condition or disorder affecting your memory shall ever affect you in Jesus' Name. We say all forms of dementia, Alzheimer's, amnesia, and memory loss are bound and any genetic disorders are halted. We speak that you are mindful, aware, and cognizant. May your memories begin to increase and expand in number. We say that all negative, haunting, and hurtful memories are replaced by positive memories that bring value to your future. We decree you are able to remember Scripture, truth, and the instructions of the Holy Spirit. We say you can remember all things you have learned through study and reading. We decree your mind and your memory are blessed and shall always function to their fullest capacity in the Name of Jesus!

SCRIPTURE

But the Comforter, which is the Holy Ghost, whom the Father will send in my name, he shall teach you all things, and bring all things to your remembrance, whatsoever I have said unto you (John 14:26).

WORD OF ENCOURAGEMENT

It's common as people get advanced in years to make jokes and quips about memory loss. However, the realities of seeing people face legitimate conditions seriously affecting one's memory are no laughing matter. Jesus promised that when the Holy Spirit came He would bring the truth of God's Word to our remembrance. If the Spirit of God can cause us to recall biblical truth, then He can also overshadow our memory as a whole. Make the habit of speaking over your mind. Speak that your memory will always function the way it is supposed to and that no condition will prevent you from recalling things. Expect your senior years to be such that you will enjoy time with your loved ones and be fully cognizant. Believe God that you will always have a sharp memory!

A COMPLETE WORK

DECLARATION

WE decree that the work that Jesus has begun in your life shall be completed and not cut short. We say everything you are meant to become and all that you are called to do shall be finished. We declare that all intimidating spirits that would make you believe you are not doing anything of significant value are bound in Jesus' Name. We say you carry upon you a finisher's anointing and that you have within you the ability to complete and finalize tasks. We declare you begin to see meaningful fruit for your labors. We say every effort to produce something profitable shall yield results. We prophesy your heavenly calling shall never be aborted and you shall finish all the work heaven has assigned you. We speak a new confidence to rest upon you regarding the good work of God being completed within you by Jesus Christ!

SCRIPTURE

Being confident of this very thing, that he which hath begun a good work in you will perform it until the day of Jesus Christ (Philippians 1:6).

WORD OF ENCOURAGEMENT

Every person on earth who serves God has a heavenly assignment. Even our gifts and callings that don't directly relate to the furtherance of the Gospel still have an eternal purpose. If you are businessperson, your line of work should still benefit the Kingdom of God in some way. We are all called to complete a work in our lives that has an eternal value. When those times come along that can make you feel like you aren't accomplishing much or just spinning your wheels, those are the times to remind yourself that the good work that Jesus has assigned you will bear fruit. He will ensure it's completed if you stay consistent and obedient. If we are confident in this fact, we will stay on track with our assignment and not give up. Prophesy that the work He began in you will be performed and perfected until the day of Jesus Christ!

AUTHORITY AND DOMINION

DECLARATION

WE decree that you rise up and take your rightful place of authority and dominion against the evils and darkness of this world. We say you shall not be intimidated by an antichrist spirit. We declare you tread boldly upon all the powers of the devil. We prophesy that you are well equipped to wage spiritual warfare and come out with a decisive win. We say that the prophetic words in your mouth are saturated with power. We say that you shall have the taste and grace upon your words to speak in places and regions that aren't receptive to the Word of God. We say you carry weightiness from the Spirit of God upon you. We say a new authority comes upon your prayer language and to your prayer life. May you walk in all the levels of dominion that Christ has established for you and may you take your rightful place of divine rule in Jesus' Name!

SCRIPTURE

Behold, I give unto you power to tread on serpents and scorpions, and over all the power of the enemy: and nothing shall by any means hurt you (Luke 10:19).

WORD OF ENCOURAGEMENT

The last thing the devil wants you to remember is who you are in Christ. He wants to make you feel powerless anytime you are confronted with difficulty or whenever you see evil in the world. His goal is to get you to back away from the rightful place of authority given to you by Jesus. Jesus has handed you and me a badge of authority and dominion to wage war on demon powers. We can wage war in prayer and then walk in this world with the confidence that the Spirit of the Lord is backing and empowering us to stand boldly for Him. Don't allow the enemy to push you around. He is under your feet and you have power over him. Rise up today in a renewed revelation of your heavenly dominion and command the powers of darkness to back off. Declare you walk in authority and dominion today in Jesus' Name!

THOUGHTS OF PURITY AND VIRTUE

DECLARATION

TODAY we speak a cleansing over your mind. We decree every thought is captive to the rule of Jesus Christ. We say all thoughts of impurity, godlessness, fear, and unbelief must dissipate. We say unhappy and undesirable imaginations must leave your mind and be replaced with that which is pure, lovely, life-giving, and filled with peace. We say that every attack of the enemy that would demonically come to bombard your thoughts with that which opposes truth and godliness are bound in the Name of Jesus. We command every evil thought to get out of your mind, be removed from your dreams, and go from your thinking. We call for a divine saturation of your mind and thoughts by the Spirit of the Lord. We decree you are able to think of a good outcome for every circumstance and that you have the capacity to imagine the light at the end of every tunnel. We prophesy that you can always picture a good report! We say your thoughts are pure, blessed, and filled with life in Jesus' Name!

SCRIPTURE

Finally, brethren, whatsoever things are true, whatsoever things are honest, whatsoever things are just, whatsoever things are pure, whatsoever things are lovely, whatsoever things are of good report; if there be any virtue, and if there be any praise, think on these things (Philippians 4:8).

WORD OF ENCOURAGEMENT

We all know how powerful our thoughts are. They ultimately dictate how we behave. If you can win the battle of the mind you are already on the road to a win. One of the most effective things you can do is exercise the ability to control your thoughts. When fearful or impure thoughts try to invade your thinking, immediately rise up against them. The best way to do that is to speak something. Your mind is disrupted from its thoughts when you start talking. If your mind is inundated with fear, immediately start speaking faith. The key is take control of your thoughts and bring them under the control of Jesus Christ.

DECLARATION FOR FRIENDS AND FAMILY

DECLARATION

WE decree today over all your friends and loved ones that they are overshadowed by the Spirit of the Lord. May the power of God rest tangibly upon them so they sense His presence. We declare they receive wisdom and revelation from the Lord. We say they hear God's voice. We prophesy they walk in divine health, live long lives, and receive God's protection. We say angels are released to encamp about them. We say your friends and loved ones shall serve the Lord and not fall away from Him. We prophesy that they walk in God's will and His divine plan for their lives. We speak that they shall find gainful employment and activity and shall enjoy life to the full. We take authority over every plot, plan, and scheme of the enemy that would try to come against your friends and loved ones. We say that devil cannot hold them in any form of bondage in Jesus' Name. We say they are well, and all is well concerning those you love!

SCRIPTURE

For God is my witness, whom I serve with my spirit in the gospel of his Son, that without ceasing I make mention of you always in my prayers (Romans 1:9).

WORD OF ENCOURAGEMENT

Prayer and declaration over the ones you love is one of kindest and most important things you can do for them. Many a lost soul came back to God because of a praying family member or friend. Don't underestimate the power of your prayers for the people in your life. It might look at times they are going the opposite direction, but never stop praying. When you pray and decree over others, there are good things taking place in the realm of the spirit that you can't see. God is moving obstacles out of the way and He is shifting hearts in the right direction. When we pray, God can cover them with His protective power. Declare over your loved ones, and regardless of what you see, know that your prayers are causing a great change and bringing help from God's throne!

IT WILL
COME TO PASS!

DECLARATION

WE decree that every prophetic word from God that has been spoken into your life shall come to pass without fail. We declare you have a steadfast confidence in the word of the Lord that has been given to you and you are able to wage a good warfare with the prophecies that have gone before you. We say that you are able to stand firm in the prophetic word and are able to discern prophetic truth. We decree all words spoken that have not lined up biblically or been proven as legitimate will not carry any weight. We speak the words from God shall be pressed through to fruition and not stopped by the enemy. We say the word of the Lord over your life concerning your prophetic future shall come to pass and shall not be aborted in the Name of Jesus. We say, "It will come to pass!"

SCRIPTURE

This charge I commit unto thee, son Timothy, according to the prophecies which went before on thee, that thou by them mightest war a good warfare (1 Timothy 1:18).

WORD OF ENCOURAGEMENT

When we think of the prophet Elijah we think of one of the most definitive prophets of Scripture. His prophecies came to pass! However, his prophetic words still had to be bathed in prayer. In First Kings 18, he *prophesied* that there would be no rain, but then in James 5:17-18 it says he *prayed fervently* that it might not rain. We see here that prophecy and prayer had to be coupled together. It's not enough to just receive a prophetic word; it needs to be covered in strong prayer. If you receive a prophecy and carelessly toss it aside, there is a tremendous chance you will never see it come to fruition. When we pray and war over the prophetic words in our life or even prophecies for a group, city, or nation, we are helping push those words through to manifestation. Decree today over the prophecies you have received and declare, "It will come to pass!"

A READY
ANSWER

DECLARATION

WE decree that within you lies the ability to give an answer to every person who would question you or ask a question of you. We say that you have the wisdom of the Lord upon your words to talk to any person who comes across your path or would ask you about things pertinent to the Kingdom of God. We prophesy that those who would come to you with hard questions will be able to receive answers from the wisdom of God that rests upon you. We speak that people shall seek you out to know the way of God and you will be able to help guide and lead them to the light. We say you have clear and decisive answers and that no spirit of confusion or perplexity shall be able to interfere with what you have to say. We say your tongue is as the pen of a ready writer able to give hope in due season and answers to a generation in need. We say the ready answers of God are in your mouth!

SCRIPTURE

But sanctify the Lord God in your hearts: and be ready always to give an answer to every man that asketh you a reason of the hope that is in you with meekness and fear (1 Peter 3:15).

WORD OF ENCOURAGEMENT

We must always remain cognizant of the fact that we are the bridge of hope for the lost or those seeking a deeper experience with the Lord. We connect them to Jesus and the Holy Spirit. Yet many are like the Queen of Sheba when she came to Solomon with hard questions, but he was able to answer them (see 2 Chron. 9:1-2). God wants us to be always ready with a clear and decisive answer for those who come to us trying to know the way of God. If we place Jesus as Lord in our hearts each day, we are better prepared to give those answers. Spend time in the Bible, pray, and prepare yourself to be a resource for people who don't know God and need answers. Ask the Lord today to put within you the ready answer for every person trying to connect to the Lord!

EXTRAORDINARY
AND UNIQUE MIRACLES

DECLARATION

WE decree that you receive and experience the unique miracles of God. Like the early church saw extraordinary miracles performed at the hands of Paul, may you encounter the miraculous works of God in your life. May you see unusual and uncommon miracles. May you be a witness of the signs and wonders that confirm God's Word in action. We say that every demonic power that would prevent you from seeing, operating in, or encountering the miraculous is bound in Jesus' Name. We speak that you interact with all the elements of His profound glory that are intended by the Holy Spirit. May unusual miracles effect your family, your personal life, occupation, finances, health, and home. We say that special miracles shall be regularly noted in your life and no man-made traditions shall keep them from manifesting. We prophesy that special and unique miracles shall be your experience and your portion in Jesus' Name!

SCRIPTURE

God did extraordinary miracles through Paul, so that even handkerchiefs and aprons that had touched him were taken to the sick, and their illnesses were cured and the evil spirits left them (Acts 19:11-12 NIV).

WORD OF ENCOURAGEMENT

It would be rare to meet a believer who didn't want to witness a notable miracle. There is something incredible that happens when you see a terminal patient healed or someone experience a financial breakthrough that transcends the odds. The thrill on any person's face when the unexpected happens in one supernatural moment is priceless. Such occurrences in Scripture are because God wants us to experience His extraordinary miracles. We can't allow religion to teach us that the Lord shies away from such things in our modern times. No! We need to stay with Scripture. We are connected to the God of special miracles and wonders and He wants to perform them in your life!

SOFT AND GENTLE WORDS

DECLARATION

WE decree that you carry a gentle and soothing word within your speech. We say that you can speak decently and tastefully in all tense conversations. We break the power of the enemy that would pressure you to defend yourself excessively or react harshly. We speak that you have the ability to maintain a calm and collected demeanor with every person you speak to. We say that wrath, anger, violence, and antagonism shall never consume you as you interact with those who would oppose you. We say you are surrounded in a gentle, mannerly spirit. We speak that those around you will be softened by your considerate behavior. May the gentle and thoughtful words that come from your mouth change your hearers for the better and may your words turn away all wrath and fighting. We say a soft and gentle word is on your lips.

SCRIPTURE

A gentle answer turns away wrath, but a harsh word stirs up anger (Proverbs 15:1 NIV).

WORD OF ENCOURAGEMENT

In the majority of conversations, the ability to speak softly and calmly can be the very element that controls how the discussion turns out. Even in heated disagreements, gentle words can bring everything back into order and keep all those involved calm. The art of offering a soft answer in these situations can come more easily for some than others, but regardless, the one who can do so is the one who typically dictates the outcome. Leaning toward the side of harshness only adds to the problem and usually creates further offenses. Additionally, offering a soft answer is also a mannerly and Christlike thing to do. It may not be always possible to bring such a gentle word in every circumstance, but it is a skill one should practice when at all possible. Ask God to help you be a person who can speak gently when needed and enable hearts to be changed and anger abated by the gracious words that come from your mouth.

NO MORE DISAPPOINTMENT

DECLARATION

WE decree you shall not live in the realm of repeated or continual disappointment. We prophesy that you shall not look at your circumstances and brace for disappointment. We break the power of all repeat patterns of letdown, setback, and disillusion in Jesus' Name. We prophesy that you will not experience negative blow after blow regarding the things you are believing for. We declare thorns and thistles are replaced with fruitful blooms. We speak that you attain results and achievement that will bring delight to your soul. We declare you see a sudden shift for the better that will boost your morale and give a new sense of determination. We decree that "disappointment" will not need to have a place in your vocabulary regarding your current situation. Disappointment is turned into delight, and we speak that you will rejoice for your season of relief has come in the Name of Jesus!

SCRIPTURE

Instead of the thorn shall come up the fir tree, and instead of the brier shall come up the myrtle tree: and it shall be to the Lord for a name, for an everlasting sign that shall not be cut off (Isaiah 55:13).

WORD OF ENCOURAGEMENT

Disappointment is different from grieving. It's not usually as tragic. It's more of that little feeling of wanting something to have turned out differently but also accepting the fact that it didn't. Learning to accept certain elements of disappointment is healthy in the sense that it makes you well balanced. However, it's not so healthy when a person is hit with repeat disappointments, particularly in one specific area. After a while it takes the wind out of your sails. Repeat blows of disappointment can be spiritual and incited by the enemy. They are also a demonic tactic intended to discourage you in prayer. Begin declaring that repeated encounters with disappointment are not allowed to have a foothold in your life or situation!

AN ENDURING PATIENCE

DECLARATION

WE decree that you possess the divine patience that heaven brings. We speak that you are steady and constant in doing the will of God. We prophesy that you are steadfast in awaiting your breakthroughs and answers to prayer. We say patience has its perfect work within you. We speak that you maintain the ability to exhibit self-control and fortitude. We break the power of that which would agitate you and frustrate you from reaching your goals. We bind the work of all demonic powers that would meddle with your steady endurance. We decree your faith shall not fail and you shall not resort to shortcuts and side roads that do not yield a bountiful harvest. We speak that you receive a divine patience from the Lord that enables you to stand strong in every promise without wavering. We say patience saturates your being and you will complete your objectives, receive answered prayer, and attain the prize of your high calling in Christ Jesus!

SCRIPTURE

For ye have need of patience, that, after ye have done the will of God, ye might receive the promise (Hebrews 10:36).

WORD OF ENCOURAGEMENT

When you mention the word *patience* in a conversation, it's often met with some humorous commentary. That is because patience is one of the hardest attributes to develop in our lives, yet it's one of the elements we most need. It is listed as one of the fruits of the Spirit (see Gal. 5:22) because a person with patience is a person who remains steady. They don't live life on a roller coaster of highs and lows, ups and downs, and they don't look for shortcuts to attain goals. A person of patience realizes that life is not a series of easy roads, but rather a long journey that requires steady choices that don't always produce visible results in a short time. Declaring patience over you will help you become that person and will enable you to see the fruit that patience brings.

THE ENEMY MUST FLEE!

DECLARATION

WE decree all the plots, plans, and schemes of the enemy must leave your life and circumstances in the authority of Jesus' Name! We prophesy that no demonic entity is allowed to hang around your home, your property, or your family. We say every evil spirit must leave your mind and your body. We say that all demonic activity must be halted. Every witchcraft curse, spell, and hex is broken by the power of God in the Name of Jesus. We draw a bloodline of the blood of Jesus around you and all that concerns you, and we say the work of evil cannot cross that line. We prophesy that where the enemy has come through as a flood, the Lord puts him to flight. We say that you rise up and resist all of the devil's activity, causing him to flee. We say to the powers of darkness, "Leave, in Jesus' Name, and never return!"

SCRIPTURE

Submit yourselves therefore to God. Resist the devil, and he will flee from you (James 4:7).

WORD OF ENCOURAGEMENT

Too often people put up with the devil hanging around. This is probably not intentional, but rather because they think some of the things going on around them are either just their own imagination or perhaps their own doing. While human activity certainly has a role in it, we cannot just assume that is the only source at work. Demons are always attempting to insert themselves in human activity. They work to drive circumstances in a different direction. Be careful not to assume that the things going awry in areas of your life are just "you." Be mindful that we don't wrestle against flesh and blood, but against demon powers (see Eph. 6:12). Make a practice of resisting the devil and commanding all demonic activity to leave. Remind the powers of darkness that your life and property are off-limits. If you feel like you are under attack, be quick to use your God-given authority and tell the enemy he has to flee!

HEAVENLY
RAINS

DECLARATION

WE decree that you begin to experience the heavenly rains of the Spirit. May you encounter the outpouring of the Spirit that causes you to be refreshed and transitioned into the next divine season for your life. We say another fruitful season comes upon you, enabling you to do things and go places that you have not before. We say your best season of growth begins to take place as a result of a spiritual rainy, well-watered season. We prophesy that the rain of God removes the impurities, leftovers, and debris from the former season. We call for the visitation of God to fall upon you as the rain, allowing you to see the intentions of God's heart, His mind, and His will. We speak against a spiritual drought and we break the work of the devouring locust and cankerworm in Jesus' Name. We decree you are transitioned out of the desert into an oasis. We declare you are able to see and hear God clearly just as you would distinctly hear the literal rain. We say God Himself comes and visits you as the rain!

SCRIPTURE

Then shall we know, if we follow on to know the Lord: his going forth is prepared as the morning; and he shall come unto us as the rain, as the latter and former rain unto the earth (Hosea 6:3).

WORD OF ENCOURAGEMENT

It's interesting how the Bible describes God's visitation as rain. It makes sense, however, because rain is unmistakable. If it's raining, you know it! You can hear, see, and even smell it. When God comes as the rain, our lives are watered by the Spirit, enabling us to grow and bear fruit. When the rain of His visitation comes, it removes the impurities and debris of a former season. His "rainy" visitation waters the desert places in our lives, which are areas where it seems we aren't producing much. God's rain softens our hearts just like natural rain softens the ground. When our hearts are soft we can receive the seed of God's Word and bear fruit—thirty-, sixty-, and one hundredfold. Ask God to visit your life as the rain!

RIGHT
ON TIME!

DECLARATION

WE decree that you always operate and function in God's perfect timing. We say in every circumstance and season that you arrive and leave with punctuality. We declare you experience timeliness both in the spiritual and the natural realms. We break the powers of tardiness, lateness, and delinquency in Jesus' Name. We prophesy that you possess the proper time-management skills in your daily activities and procrastination is broken from you. We also speak that you manage time correctly in spiritual things and we say that you will not hold on to a former season beyond it's time. We declare you transition into the next chapter of your life right on time. We declare that you hear the movement and inner workings of God's clock and are skilled to walk in step with Him. We prophesy that you are able to see time as God does. We also declare no more overdue blessings and breakthroughs and we break the spirit of delay! We say that nothing in your life is behind schedule and everything is on time!

SCRIPTURE

Look carefully then how you walk, not as unwise but as wise, making the best use of the time, because the days are evil (Ephesians 5:15-16 ESV).

WORD OF ENCOURAGEMENT

Making good use of our time is something that must be proactively practiced. Whenever a new year comes, people often begin by working on their schedule in an effort to be better organized. Timeliness, naturally speaking, is important to success. There are countless reasons why punctuality is so important—a couple being that it's respectful to others and also puts you at an advantage. But it's not just important to be punctual in the natural realm. We need to be in step with God's timing. We can't get ahead of God or lag behind Him. The way to ensure we walk in God's perfect timing is by declaring it and asking God to reveal His perfect timing in everything we do. Believe God today that you will never be too early, never be late, and *always* be right on time!

PROMOTE HIS
GOODNESS

WE decree you are able to see the good in all situations and circumstances. We speak that you will never be inclined to take the pessimistic approach. We say that you always look around you with an optimistic outlook. We speak that you don't emphasize the problem, but you are focused on the answer. We prophesy that you can look through every dark cloud and see the goodness of your God! We break any mental images of doom and gloom in Jesus' Name. We say that you look at this world through the eyes of God's redemptive plan and His mercy that triumphs over judgement. We say you see the good, promote the good, and show His goodness to the world. We declare that you are immersed in God's goodness to you and your family. We say that an anointing comes upon you to advocate everywhere you go that God is good and His mercy endures forever!

SCRIPTURE

O give thanks unto the Lord; for he is good; for his mercy endureth for ever (1 Chronicles 16:34).

WORD OF ENCOURAGEMENT

Anyone can talk about how bad things are and emphasize how messed up the world is or how bad life is going. But it takes an anointing from God to look past the dark clouds and see the good. Sure, there is sin in the world and God's judgement will be exacted upon it, but we aren't called to spend our days emphasizing that alone. We are called to promote His goodness. As long as God's Spirit is here on earth He has a redemptive plan of hope for humanity. He has a redemptive plan for you. God wants us to see His goodness at work in every situation. Some may call it optimism, but it's really the ability to see His goodness amidst turmoil. Remember, no matter how dark it seems, if you look for it, you can see God's goodness at work. You can see His hand involved, so always remember to promote His goodness!

ABOUT
BRENDA KUNNEMAN

B RENDA KUNNEMAN pastors Lord of Hosts Church in Omaha, Nebraska with her husband, Hank. She is a writer and teacher who ministers nationally and internationally, seeing lives change through the prophetic word and ministry in the Holy Spirit coupled with a balanced, relevant message. Together, she and her husband also host a weekly TV program, *New Level with Hank and Brenda*, on Daystar Television Network.